Empathy & Compassionate Action

Issues and Exercises

a guided workbook for clients in treatment

by Laren Bays &

Robert Freeman-Longo

NEARI Press

Cover Design: Whitman Communications, Inc.

ISBN: 1-929657-04-8

Order from:

Whitman Distribution
10 Water Street, PO Box 1220
Lebanon, NH 03766
(603) 448-0037
(800) 353-3730

Published by:

NEARI Press
70 North Summer Street
Holyoke, MA 01040
413-532-1713

$12.00
Payable in U.S. funds only
Bulk discounts available

Acknowledgments

We would like to thank Stacey Bird, Sharon Covington, Robin Jones, Michael Llach, Bill Marshall, and Anita Schlank for their invaluable feedback on this workbook. Most of all, we would like to thank the survivors of sexual abuse who have helped us understand their trauma and have shared with us their recovery process.

Contents

Introduction

CONGRATULATIONS AND THANK YOU for acquiring *Empathy & Compassionate Action*. The best news is that you can develop empathy, even if you feel that you've never had it before. You can learn how to act compassionately, even though you've seriously hurt others in your life by physically, emotionally, or sexually abusing them!

This workbook, along with several others, was developed to help people who have sexual behavior problems. We strongly recommend that before beginning this workbook you read and do the exercises in the workbook *Who Am I and Why Am I in Treatment?* Completing the next two workbooks *Why Did I Do It Again?* and *How Can I Stop?* will help you understand and stop your hurtful behavior, while this workbook helps you develop *positive* attitudes and behaviors toward others. Before you can work on developing empathy, you need to understand why you sexually abuse others and how you can stop. Trying to develop empathy while fantasizing about or committing rape, child molestation, or other sexually abusive acts is impossible!

The other workbooks teach you about the thoughts, feelings, and behaviors that make up your sexual abuse cycle. You also learn about risk factors for sexual abuse, and what you can do to change your behavior to stop sexually offending. If you are going to develop empathy, you must first take responsibility for your sexually abusive behavior. This means you cannot deny or minimize your sexual offenses. If you insist you have never hurt anyone, it is unlikely that you will ever understand compassion. In denial, you are erasing from your thoughts the all-too-real pain of your victim who deserves empathy.

In this book we will discuss empathy. No one is completely empathic and sensitive all the time. We all fail far too often; that is the human condition. Even though we know we'll never be perfect we still need to strive for an important goal. When we use the North Star to guide us, we never expect to reach the star, but it can be very helpful steering us along our path. Some people never look up and notice where they are headed. We hope that you will choose to direct your life toward the bright star of empathy.

Empathy can be learned, but to learn it you must be willing to practice. Even people with highly developed empathy must use it frequently. When they don't, their ability to feel

Professionals and others do things to try to cure us ...

We heal ourselves. —*anonymous*

empathy and compassion weakens and dries up. This workbook provides you with many opportunities to practice empathy and compassion through assignments and exercises. When you do not understand an assignment, ask your therapist, group, or a close friend for help. Do not write in this workbook—use a special notebook. Then review your assignments with your therapist, group, or a friend.

We strongly recommend that you join a treatment program for sexual abusers. However, if specialized treatment is not available, find a therapist to support you in doing this difficult — but rewarding — life changing work. Some abusers must work through the book on their own (which we do not recommend), because no treatment of any kind is available. If you are in this situation, it is very important to share your assignments with someone you trust to give you accurate, honest feedback. This person must be able to handle hearing difficult stuff and not reject you. This person must NOT be a potential victim, and must NOT be helping you continue to victimize others. This person would have to be understanding and willing to learn all about your abusive behavior. Finding someone like that is a very tough assignment, but it is a first serious step on the road to changing your life.

The short version of why you should read this book goes something like this:

1. You have done things that hurt people: you have done bad things, but you are not a bad person —that is not your identity.
2. You have hurt other people because that's how you learned to meet your emotional needs.
3. You may have learned to meet your needs in these hurtful ways because you were abused physically, emotionally, or sexually, or simply by learning from your environment. Even when this is true, it is not an excuse for hurting others.
4. You can learn how to respond to situations, relate to people, and meet your needs in ways that don't hurt other people.
5. Learning to relate to others and meet your needs without hurting other people isn't easy, but it is rewarding—it maintains your community standing, raises your self-esteem, and may even help you make real friends.
6. Learning empathy, to feel how others feel, is part of learning to relate to others and meet your needs without hurting someone else. Reading this book and doing the exercises will help you learn empathy.
7. YOU — AND ONLY YOU — HAVE THE POWER TO CHANGE THE WAY YOU RELATE TO OTHER PEOPLE AND THE WORLD.

We congratulate you on your efforts to change your life for the better. We wish you courage and determination in carrying out your treatment program and in completing this workbook.

Laren Bays
Oregon

Rob Freeman-Longo
Vermont

1.

What is Empathy?

EMPATHY IS FEELING FOR OTHERS. It means being able to share their joys and suffering. It is giving of your emotional self without needing to get something back from the other person. If you have ever cried at a movie, or felt tearful listening to someone talk about a problem, it was probably because you put yourself in the shoes of the person you were listening to. In some way, you felt someone else's distress and pain. That is empathy.

Other ways to think about and describe empathy include: feeling compassion, being sympathetic, understanding, being sensitive, and identifying with others' feelings and situations.

Words that do not describe empathy include: self-centered, harsh, indifferent, resistant, discouraging, unsupportive, impatient, angry, inconsiderate, hostile, irritated, selfish, mean, abusive, cynical.

Being empathic doesn't just happen to you. It is not something you simply "do" or learn in a few minutes or a few days. It must be learned by feeling deeply and paying very close attention to the real feelings of others (and not using your attention to

groom them as potential victims!). It must be developed and cultivated over time. It is like growing a garden. After the seeds are sown, the budding plants must be tended carefully: fertilized, watered, weeded, and watched for insects. If you do all this, and pay close attention, you will end up with strong, healthy plants, and a good harvest. When you just throw some seeds on the ground, ignore them, and come back five weeks later, you will have a garden of weeds.

Why bother with empathy?

You don't have enough empathy. If you were a truly empathic person before you sexually abused others, you would not have raped, molested, or sexually abused your victims. It would have been much more difficult for you to hurt your victims after looking them in the eyes and understanding what they felt.

You may have occasional flashes of feeling concern and caring for people that you know. But either it doesn't happen very often, or it's always combined with figuring out how you can use the situation or the feelings to get something you want. For example, you might feel enough concern for your mother to do errands for her occasionally. But another time, you're stealing money from her purse. Or you may pretend that you are concerned about a friend's sick child by picking up medicine at the drug store, when in the back of your mind you're thinking, "Good, now I can ask her to babysit my kid next weekend."

On the other hand, you may be a very empathic person—until something happens and you get angry or sexually aroused. Then all that empathy drains away, and you don't even see the person in front of you any more. That person is no longer a real live human being like you, with feelings and fears, and all you focus on is your feelings and needs. You may be able to feel empathy for some people and not for others. Sometimes the people we have the least empathy for are those most like us. Sometimes we have no empathy for people who are very different from us.

There are other feelings that you might mistake for empathy, such as feeling bad about yourself, being afraid of the consequences of your actions, being worried about yourself. A good therapist and/or a treatment group can really help you sort out your feelings and learn what true empathy is.

People who go out of their way to help others probably do it because they feel empathy. They understand on a gut level, a feeling level, what other people go through, and they want to help. Many—but not all—people in the helping professions, such as doctors, social workers, counselors and spiritual leaders, joined their professions because they saw how much pain and suffering there was in the world, and they wanted to do something to help make it better. The experience of going to see a doctor who has empathy for your situation is a good example. Seeing a doctor who really cares about your problems, listens to what you have to say, and treats you respectfully is very different from going to a doctor who doesn't spend time with you and is only interested in making money.

To cultivate empathy requires caring for and respecting others. But to care for someone else, you have to respect yourself and care for yourself. It is hard to give others something that you don't have. If you work hard on changing your life and have the support of your treatment group, this workbook can help you learn to feel better about yourself by learning how to care for others.

Deep down, we're all the same.

All of us want to feel happy, and we all want to avoid suffering. We all suffer from the loss of what we like and love: people move away, our health takes a turn for the worse, what we build begins to wear away, and all living things eventually die. No matter how high we get, we always come down. We may have money today, but the bills come and the money goes. No matter how much control we think we have over life, things happen and we begin to lose the illusion that we're in control.

This does not mean that people are not accountable for their behavior! There are three things we can be in control of—our own feelings, our own thoughts, and our own behaviors. We are all responsible for everything we do, whether it is an act of kindness or a criminal offense. We cannot blame our past for what we do today and tomorrow. Thinking that you have the right to "make up for it" or be excused for bad behavior because you have suffered is a serious mistake. Past suffering is a good reason to take care with each thing you do. Doing your best will help you avoid unnecessary pain in the future and will give you more chances to enjoy your life.

Given this human condition, what can we do to make life meaningful? There are many answers to this question, but most of them are found in the spiritual traditions and are outside the scope of this workbook. However, having empathy and helping others is one way to find meaning in your life.

Take the time to look at your life and the lives of others around you. Realize that others are human, with real problems, just like you. Everyone is in the same boat trying to hold it all together without feeling more distress, anxiety, grief, and pain than necessary. A deep understanding of this leads to empathy and respect for others.

Do you want to be bitter or better?

Look at Carl's situation:

> Carl was sent to prison for a year. Because he was sent to prison, he lost his job. Eventually his wife left him. Carl came out of prison feeling bitter and resentful. After his release, Carl had two possible directions: He could try to get even, or he could make the best of the situation and build a new life for himself.
>
> For a long time he planned how he could get even with "society." He knew places he could steal from and get away with it. He thought out in detail all the things he could do to make life hard for his ex-wife. But as Carl kept going to AA meetings, a requirement of his parole, he kept hearing the message that he needed to let go of his fantasies of revenge. Revenge would in the end make him feel worse, not better. It kept him tied in to the negative things in his life, instead of allowing him to move on and rebuild.
>
> Gradually he realized that he needed to try to make the best of it. He would need to get a new job, hard enough for an excon without trying to cover up new thefts. He needed to set some positive goals, ones that would keep him out of jail. Listening to other guys in the meeting who had been divorced helped him realize that he needed to feel and express his grief, pain, and anger about his exwife's leaving him while he was in jail. Only when he had worked out at least some of his anger at her would he be able to safely start dating other women. His other choice was to hold onto his anger and let it fester inside him, poisoning any chances he might have to build a new family that would be supportive and loving.

Which path do you think would lead Carl to a better life in the future?

Some people try to escape the distress of the human condition, unfortunate circumstances such as poverty, or the consequences of bad choices they have made, by harming others. They may be afraid to be without money. Their understandable fear of being without money may make stealing seem more attractive and more possible than getting a job; so they choose to steal. If they are afraid of their loneliness or their vulnerability, they may try to escape it by stealing sex (through sexual abuse or rape) or attempting to control others.

Sex, money, and personal power are the things most often stolen by people who want to think they are strong. They have very little empathy because they think only about themselves. They think they are different from and more important than everyone else. They are selfish—if they see something they want, they steal it. Stealing is not about being powerful—it is about feeling powerless.

Sometimes people steal things that can't be seen. For example, if a man is married to a woman who is more successful in her job than he is, he may attempt to steal her pride by putting her down and making unreasonable demands. By trying to control her, he affects her ability to do her job well, and he slows her down. Because he feels inadequate, he mistakenly thinks he is better off with a wife who is weaker than he is. If his children are smart in school, he may try to steal their confidence by calling them names, telling them they are getting uppity, or too big for their britches, and that they are insulting him by doing well in school. By trying to control them in this way, he kills their curiosity and creativity.

Unfortunate and distressed situations you experience won't change until you make a decision to take control of your life. Learning about empathy is one important step toward having real strength. If you have no empathy, you are likely to blame others for your problems. Each time you blame someone else, you give up the power to change your life.

Feel for yourself so you can feel for others.

Think back to a sexually abusive act you committed and what you did to your victim. Maybe you felt remorse, guilt, or shame after you committed your crime. In this case, these uncomfortable feelings are good. Feeling intensely bad after you have done wrong or been hurt is the start of empathy.

Recall a time when you felt the worst. It may have been when you knew you failed badly, were put down, arrested, or went bankrupt. Remember how horrible you felt? Others feel equally badly when terrible things happen to them.

Now think back to a time when something was happening to your body that you didn't like, and you felt powerless to stop it. It may have been a relative who insisted on kissing you when you were a child, a doctor's examination, a strip search by a prison guard, or a dentist who did not care about your pain when filling your cavity. Remember how it felt to have someone invading your physical being and personal boundaries? Others feel the same.

Now remember or imagine being the victim of a crime. By remembering the intensity and pain of your past humiliations, failures, and hurts, you can understand what it might be like to have a crime committed against you. Now you can begin to imagine how your victims felt. Victims feel intensely hurt, invaded, and upset.

Even when you can recognize how much pain, sorrow or depression you feel about your crimes, remember that your victims feel even worse. Working on appreciating how others feel by remembering your own similar experiences is a way to begin to feel empathy.

Keep in mind that the focus of empathy is not how *you* feel—it is how *others* feel. But the only way you can know this is to feel deeply yourself, and then *put yourself in the other person's place*. If you can feel for yourself, you are on the path to learning how to feel for others.

When you have real empathy, you feel compassion for others' struggles and you want to help them with their problems. When you have empathy, you don't add your weakness to their problems. You take responsibility for yourself and your actions.

Empathy building can be tough on your emotions.

As you learn about empathy, the way you look at your past actions is likely to change. Looking at what you've done may make you feel depressed, angry with yourself, guilty, ashamed or embarrassed. This is a necessary, healthy step in developing empathy.

During times when all you feel are huge negative feelings and thoughts, you may want to give up and drown your problems with alcohol, sex, or excitement. Giving up may bring temporary relief from distressing feelings, but it will not solve your problems. As you work on your treatment, you will begin to feel better. You can rebuild your self-esteem and your life on a foundation of honesty.

Sometimes abusers feel suicidal when they truly understand the pain and suffering they have caused other people. **If you do find yourself thinking about suicide, planning how you could do it and when, you *must* tell someone—call a suicide prevention hotline—and get professional help from a therapist, counselor, or clergy person before continuing to work through this book.**

A therapist can help you look at your suicidal feelings while helping you plan how to stay safe. Change is scary! With professional help, you may discover that feeling suicidal could be a last-ditch effort to hang on to your old destructive behaviors, a way to keep being self-centered, an expression of self-pity, or a way to avoid looking at your feelings or taking responsibility for the hurtful things you have done. Remember that committing suicide could result in a victim feeling responsible for your death. Sexually victimized children are especially likely to blame themselves for getting the abuser into trouble. Adding pain to a victim's experience by committing suicide is not a form of empathy. The main thing you can do for your victims is to change your thoughts, feelings and behaviors so you don't revictimize them or victimize others.

Self-pity is not empathy.

Feeling sad for someone else's misfortune is a form of empathy. Feeling sorry for yourself is not. Feeling sorry for yourself is an *enabling* behavior: it allows you to look past the effects of your actions and continue the behavior that got you into trouble in the first place. Self-pity can keep you thinking you are a victim and not the abuser.

Many abusers confuse self-pity with disgust for what they have done. Abusers feel sorry for themselves after they are arrested. They worry about their jobs and what their friends and families will think about them. They worry about going to prison and what might happen in prison. While these concerns are legitimate, they are also self-centered. Those worries are based in self-

pity and let abusers avoid thinking about the pain and expense their victims are suffering through or how what they have done affects their wives and families, or the families of their victims.

Self-pity prevents you from developing empathy. Self-pity keeps you self-centered and does not help you change and grow. When you feel sorry for yourself, you blame others for the consequences of your own actions. The more you let yourself feel self-pity, the deeper you sink into the pit of self-focused anger and resentment. It is like trying to drive a car that is stuck in the mud: The more you spin the wheels, the deeper into the mud you go. The only way through is to get out, take an honest look at the problem, and make a decision about how you can solve it.

Self-disgust, shame, and guilt can motivate you to change.

Self-disgust is different from self-pity. Disgust about the abusive acts you have committed, how it has hurt and damaged others, and how you have wasted your life is appropriate and realistic. This kind of negative feeling can be a step in the right direction, if you use it to motivate yourself to change and improve your life.

Feeling shame and guilt can lead either to self-pity or healthy disgust. Shame is feeling bad about who you are. Guilt is feeling bad about what you have done by sexually abusing or otherwise hurting another human being. When you feel truly ashamed of who you have become, or truly guilty about your behavior, it can motivate you. Feeling shame or guilt without a desire to better yourself is just another form of self-pity.

It takes hard work to avoid falling into the pity-pot. You have to believe in yourself and your ability to change. You can turn your feelings of shame and guilt into strength from looking at yourself honestly and making a commitment to create a better life for yourself. A person who likes himself and is comfortable with his own feelings is more likely to be empathic with other people.

Everyone benefits from empathy.

As you develop your capacity for empathy, it will change the way you relate to and treat other people. With empathy, you will find yourself considering their well-being. Empathy will be one more coping strategy that can help you reduce your urges to assault or sexually abuse someone, or reduce the likelihood that you will act on those urges.

Sometimes you need to put the needs of others ahead of your own. It is not always healthy or in your best interests to put yourself first. For example, if you think of the needs of your family first and yourself second, your family will be much more peaceful, which is good for you. When others' needs are met, yours are often met as well.

For another example, when you help an unskilled person who is surviving on welfare to learn a trade, the person feels better, you feel good, and society and the person both benefit financially. If you are a teacher and you understand a student's state of mind, you can teach better, the student learns more, and you benefit from a positive experience. When the administrators of a prison understand some of the boredom and frustration the inmates experience, they will often start recreational, educational, and treatment programs. When they do, inmates may have access to healthier, more meaningful activities, and the prison has fewer problems. Everyone wins.

Understanding the meaning of empathy and its benefits is taking a major step forward in your recovery. Treatment is not always easy, but the returns are long-lasting if you work hard.

Chapter 1 Assignments

∞ Do not write in this workbook ∞

1.1   How would you define empathy? What would you do differently in your life if you had more empathy?

1.2   List at least five people (use their first names only and list what their relationship is to you, such as a friend, your sister-in-law, a neighbor) who have problems that are as great or greater than yours. The people on your list might have severe problems with: mental health, physical health, finances, children, parents, spouses, work, basic survival, or being harassed by someone.

        How do their problems affect their lives? If they did not have these problems, what could they do that they can't do now?

1.3   What is it like to grow old (over 65)? Either write from your experience, ask someone you know, or read about it. In a way, this is thinking about your own future: if you do not die of disease, accident, or violence, you will experience growing old.

1.4   Try to put yourself in your parents' shoes. What is a typical day like for each of them? What is hard and what is easy for them? What do they like and dislike? What do you think they feel and think during the day? What would they normally think about you? (If your parents are not alive, write about a time when they were, or write about another close relative for this exercise.)

1.5   What is your personal definition of courage? Is your definition healthy or unhealthy? Why?

1.6   How could a rapist, burglar, child molester, or extortionist be a weak and fearful person? Try to imagine what kind of fears, unmet needs, anger, and delusions might drive such people. If they were truly responsible for themselves and cared about others, would they continue committing their crimes? Why or why not?

1.7   How would you know if you were in a self-pitying state? What would be the signs? How would you act? What is one thing you could do to help yourself get out of the self-pitying state?

1.8   What are 10 things in your life that you wish you had done? What are 10 things in your life that you feel disgusted with yourself because you did them?

1.9   Now look back in your life and name 10 things you have done that you feel proud of.

1.10   List the difficulties you might have as you work on developing empathy. What are the things about you, your feelings and attitudes, your circumstances and life situation right now that might be roadblocks to developing empathy?

1.11   Using the figure below, think back to times in your life when you could have felt empathy but did not. Does the figure make sense? Give examples of how you have either engaged in self-pity or made a deliberate decision to not feel empathy.

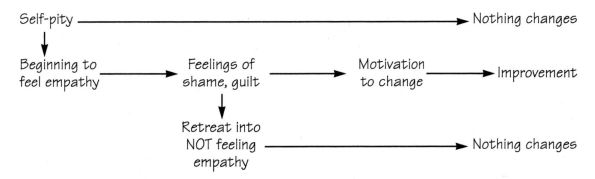

1.12   Give examples of 10 different times this week you thought of yourself first and either ignored or considered others a distant second. Give the same example only once. (You had many more than 10 incidents, guaranteed!)

1.13   Give five examples of times in your life you helped others with no thought of reward or personal advantage, beyond feeling good within yourself for having helped.

1.14   If you learned to be empathic, how would your family or friends benefit? How could you benefit?

2.

How My Sexual Behavior Affects Others

THERE IS ONE VERY IMPORTANT REASON for you to be in treatment. You have sexually abused and harmed people. **Having no more victims is the goal of treatment.** Having *no* more victims means you are in recovery. Having *any* more victims means you have failed your treatment and yourself. Empathy becomes part of your plan to prevent yourself from acting on any future urges you may have toward sexually abusing someone. When you begin to practice empathy, you will understand how it feels to be tricked, lied to, and used, and you won't want to be the person who caused that kind of pain to someone else.

Empathy improves the quality of your life. As you develop empathy, you will feel good about other people and care for them—and those caring feelings will help you feel good about yourself. When you feel the beginnings of confidence in yourself, realize that you can have satisfying adult relationships, and know your work on yourself is important, you will understand that controlling and hurting others is not the only way to get your needs met.

It is important to do well in treatment and improve your life skills. Remember that your progress is not based on your level of satisfaction with yourself and your life. It is not based on how deeply you feel, or how well you understand that what you did is wrong. **The only true measure of your progress and success in treatment is your not having one more victim**. Developing empathy will help you reach the goal of having no more victims.

It is very important that you understand how painful and damaging sexual abuse is to the victims. This chapter is about the effects of sexual abuse on all victims. When you read it, imagine that someone you really care about was victimized in these ways by someone else. As you develop empathy, come back and read it again while thinking about the people you have hurt by your behavior. You may have been victimized by someone in your own childhood, and reading this chapter may be painful for you because it brings up feelings and memories you have worked hard to ignore or forget. But remember these two important points:

1) being indifferent to others or thinking that your pain is greater than theirs is setting yourself up to commit more sexual abuse; and

2) being in touch with your own pain is one step on the way to understanding others' pain.

The effects of sexual abuse go deep and last a lifetime.

You may feel sorry for yourself because you are in prison or on probation for your crime. Whether you are on probation for two years or in prison for 10 years, at least you know your release date. Sexual abuse victims, on the other hand, have an indeterminate sentence—without help they serve a life sentence of shame, pain, and limited options. Feeling sorry for yourself because you are experiencing the consequences of your own actions will get in the way of your feeling empathy.

The effects on each particular victim of sex abuse vary, but no victim goes unharmed. The damage is deep and much of it never goes away. Victims of sexual abuse may be emotionally or mentally disabled with: depression, rage, anxiety, uncontrollable terror, feelings of powerlessness, sleep disorders, nightmares, flashbacks, sexual problems, prostitution, eating disorders, alcoholism, drug abuse, lack of self-esteem, lack of confidence, inability to motivate themselves, inability to say no, confusion, guilt, shame, self-hatred, self-

mutilation, physical illness, excessive worry about health, withdrawal from loved ones, isolation, and suicide.

The abuse can affect victims' lifestyles in many ways. Some victims are too terrified to live in their own homes or neighborhoods, and move when they can. Others are so uncomfortable around the type of individual who abused them (anyone with a moustache, all men) that they avoid going certain places or meeting people who remind them in any way of the person who abused or raped them. Victims may fear the dark or being alone. Some can't brush their teeth or stand to go to the dentist because they were forced into fellatio. They may lose their families, friends, jobs, and joyful activities, such as running or dancing, because of the abuse.

Sexual abuse also physically harms victims' bodies. Forced penetration, whether it is vaginal, anal, or oral, can tear the victim's skin. Physical restraint, struggle, or assault (such as tying, holding down, cutting, burning, or hitting victims) can damage skin and muscle, dislocate joints, break bones, suffocate, and kill. Usually victims fear for their lives. They may be so terrified that they vomit, urinate or defecate. During sexual assault, some victims get pregnant and/or contract sexually transmitted diseases, such as hepatitis, chlamydia, and the AIDS virus, which is generally considered fatal.

Going to court to testify against an offender who is in denial is described by many victims as similar to being sexually abused all over again. Recounting the assault stirs up all the feelings and memories. Seeing the abuser in court is frightening and creates intense anxiety. When the offender's lawyer accuses the victim of lying, it hurts deeply and creates an undeserved sense of shame.

Though you will never know *exactly* how your victims have been affected, you may have some sense of these emotions from your own experiences. If you were abused as a child in some way, you may be aware of how that experience still affects you. If you were beaten by a parent and told that you were stupid or worthless, you may feel worthless to this day. You may still be carrying around anger toward your parent(s) that you've had for years. If you were sexually abused by someone in childhood, you may have tried to forget it or attempted to disconnect from the feelings those memories bring up. But somewhere inside, you remember how bad it felt, and you can begin to understand what an effect it has had on the rest of your life. Being abused is never an excuse for abusing someone else. But it does give you an idea of the feelings other victims also have about being sexually abused, feelings and effects that will bother them for the rest of their lives.

In a good treatment program, you will learn in detail about the effects of sexual abuse on your yourself and on victims. If you are going to develop empathy and have no more victims, you must understand what victims have experienced and what they will continue to experience as a result of being sexually abused.

Hell is for children.

In the U.S. about one in four children experience some kind of sexual abuse before the age of 18. Even more children are physically and emotionally abused or neglected. Those are the awful numbers, the horrible reality behind Pat Benatar's song, "Hell is for Children."

Children from every social and economic background are abused. White, Black, Asian, Latino, rich, poor, sophisticated, simple, smart, athletic, and disabled children all are the victims of sex crimes. Young children, older children, eldest, youngest and middle children all are among the abused. Plain, beautiful, sickly, healthy, fat and underweight children all show up when abused children are counted. It is not up to these children to stop the abuse. It is up to adults, and the place to start is with yourself.

Sex crimes against children include: exposing yourself (showing your genitals, or sexual parts), fondling (touching their genitals or breasts, or having them touch yours), anal intercourse, vaginal intercourse, masturbating on or in front of the victim, fellatio (oral sex on a male), cunnilingus (oral sex on a female), having sex with someone else in front of children, having children have sex with each other in front of you, and exposing children to pornography. Children are the victims of every kind of sex crime. When we use the term "molestation," it refers to any of these crimes.

About half of incest victims are forced into intercourse; that is, they are raped. About 80 percent of all incest victims are subjected to verbal threats, 45 percent are beaten or excessively punished, and 30 percent need medical care.

Incest abusers tend to repeat their hurtful acts on children and often continue for years. Many incest perpetrators have more than one victim. Child molesters who abuse outside the family usually have many, many victims, perhaps hundreds. That's a lot of pain, a lot of wonderful human potential stunted, and way too many deaths from suicide, drug and alcohol abuse, and eating disorders.

No child wants to be abused.

Child victims of sexual abuse are tricked, bribed, punished, seduced, or forced into being sexual with adults. Many abusers twist logic into pretzel shapes because they are working so hard to convince themselves and their victims that the children were the cause of the molestation. Imagine a 170-pound man being "forced" into being

sexual by a 60-pound girl. A child cannot force an adult to do something that the adult does not want to do. Could a child trick or force an adult into buying her a new bike if the adult did not want to? On the other hand, how easy would it be for an adult to trick or force a child into buying something that she did not want?

Some sex abusers say that the children they abused "wanted it." But truly wanting something means having some idea of the consequences of getting it. A child who wants love or truly needs attention may think that the way to get it is to do what an abuser wants. But the child does not understand that the consequence to herself is pain. Even if it seemed to you that a child wanted to have sex and seemed to enjoy it, it is still your responsibility to know that sex with children is both wrong and harmful to the child. You are the adult—you are the one who must think about consequences for the child *and* for yourself. How Taylor handled his situation is a case in point: you can read his story on the next page.

Of course, it is not easy to think about consequences when you are sexually aroused. First you have to *notice* that you are aroused. Then you have to remember that you're in a situation that's dangerous for you *and* for the child. Next you have to get out of the situation as quickly as possible without hurting or being sexual with the child. Thinking about consequences and acting to prevent harm even when you're under stress shows maturity, responsibility, and empathy.

If someone offered you a free trip to Hawaii, would you want it? Probably; most of us would. But if you found out when you got there that you had to pay high hotel rates and a huge "processing fee" to get back home, you would have doubts about having accepted the "free trip."

Children don't have the life experience to understand the long-term consequences of the decisions they make. So even if they know what sex is and say they want to have sex, they are not saying yes to the *real* consequences of sex between children and adults: betrayal of trust, lies, secrets, threats, fear of abandonment, learning difficulties, stunted emotions, mental illness, sexually transmitted diseases, possible pregnancy, and sexual problems as adults. Forcing a child to do something that will lead to this kind of suffering is not empathic.

Think back to your own childhood and you will remember that adults have a lot of power over children. When you were young, you had to do what adults told you to, from taking out the garbage, to doing your homework, to taking a bath. Children almost never have the option of saying no. And if you can't say no, saying yes has no meaning. If a six-foot-tall police officer with a gun asks a man if he wants to be sodomized, would the answer "yes" con-

Taylor

Thinking about it later, Taylor could figure out how he got into the situation, but at the time he was surprised. He was walking home from the bus after work, when this 5-year-old girl walked toward him along the park fence. "Hey Mister," she said, "Can you help me? I'm lost."

He just wanted to help the kid get home—it was getting dark, and no little kid should be out on the streets after dark. "Sure," he said. "I'll help you. How'd you get lost, anyway?"

The little girl put her hand in his. "My brother told me I was being a slowpoke, and he left without me. He's gonna get it when I get home and tell my mother."

Taylor started feeling warmth in his groin, but tried to ignore it. "Do you know your address?"

As she told him the street address, Taylor could no longer deny that he was becoming aroused being around this little girl. He thought about how he would feel if his daughter was brought home after dark by a strange man. From his arousal, Taylor knew he was in trouble. He was probably violating his parole conditions just talking to this kid. He began to sweat. Her home wasn't far from where they stood, just a few blocks, but there were vacant lots on the way.

"This is bad for her and bad for me. How do I get us out of this?" Taylor thought to himself. Half a block behind him was a corner store, he remembered. He walked the girl there and asked the clerk to keep an eye on her while he went to the phone booth across the parking lot.

He called his therapist, explained the situation, and together they figured out that he should have the storekeeper find out the girl's last name and phone number and call her parents to come get her. Taylor talked to the clerk and left the store, but he watched from across the street for the parents to arrive.

Later that week, he talked about the situation in his group. "I felt so bad for her," he said, "She was little, lost, and it was dark. But I knew it was bad for her to be with me. So I took her to the nearest public place and tried to make sure she'd be safe. And that kept me safe, too."

vince you that the man truly wants sex with him? Adults know they have more power than children. Adults have to take responsibility for having that power by not using it for harm. Being responsible for the power you have over children means never engaging in sex with children, ever.

Some children who have been abused in the past may act sexual around adults because they have been taught that this is the way to get attention and affection. It is always the responsibility of the adult not to go along or take advantage of the child and to try to get help for the child from a therapist.

Being sexually abused as a child is devastating.

Victims of childhood sexual abuse experience some or all of the following:

1. **Distrust of others and themselves.** Some of the deepest damage comes from abuse that is disguised as love, affection, tenderness or comfort, or when an adult who otherwise acts loving abuses a child. These children learn that love means being used. When children are hurt by people they thought could be trusted, or those who told the children to trust them, they learn that trust leads to betrayal and loss.

   Some abusers also destroy the child's ability to trust by telling child victims lies about the people who truly *are*

trustworthy (for example, other close family members). They may say to their victims that their mothers don't love them, or that the victims' brothers and sisters would be jealous and hurt them if they knew about the "special" games, the abuse. Victims are typically told not to let anyone know about the abuse. All of this leaves the victims with no trust in themselves to make decisions. These children may be so confused that they never trust anyone again.

Adults who were sexually abused in childhood may be left with fear of even gentle sex, tension around secrets, the inability to make choices, distrust of their own feelings about themselves and other people, and fear of others in general. Without trust, there is no place to really rest, ever.

2. **Terror and anxiety.** When abuse happens in places that can't be avoided, such as in their homes, schools, neighborhoods, or relatives' houses, they may live every minute of their childhoods in a state of trapped terror. Repeated abuse leaves victims feeling anxious and powerless to stop the pain, no matter what they do.

Sexual abuse victims often are afraid that they will be killed by the abuse itself or by the abuser. Child molesters often threaten to kill their victims if they tell anyone. The victims may become afraid to say no to anything in their lives. Some victims become *hyper-vigilant* (always nervously watchful), always keeping track of things such as who is behind them or where the doors are in a room. They experience fears of many kinds: of the dark, being alone, being with others, of sleep, nightmares, and flashbacks. Being always afraid and watchful takes up most of the energy these children should be able to spend learning in school, playing children's games, finding friends, or exploring the world. These experiences can torture the victims deeply for decades, just like flashbacks to the war in Vietnam can ruin the lives of veterans.

In adulthood, these fears may prevent victims of childhood sexual abuse from participating in certain activities, taking a job, or living in a particular area.

3. **Shame, guilt, and self-hatred.** Abused children often think that the reason they are being sexually abused is because there is something wrong with them. Girls may feel (because the offender tells them so) that they are being abused because they are pretty or handsome. Victims may hate their attractiveness because they think it has caused their problems.

Sometimes the offender may make the child believe that he is doing him or her a favor by being sexual with him or her because he or she is so ugly that no one else could possibly want to be a friend or have a relationship. Incest abusers often do this to prevent their victims from making friends with or dating boys or girls their own age. This has a devastating effect on the child's self image.

Child victims may feel they have been forever damaged by what was done to them. They often feel intense shame because of what the abusers made them do, or because of how their friends and family reacted when they found out. They may feel guilty because they mistakenly believe that what they did (not what the abusers did) caused the disturbances in their families' lives. The worst shame and guilt occur when adult abusers unfairly blame their victims for the abuse. And even beyond that, girls know that they've already lost their virginity, and boys wonder if they are gay because they were abused.

4. **Alienation from their bodies.** Child victims of sexual abuse that is manipulative (emotionally violent), but not physically violent, may hate their bodies for responding positively to the abuse that damaged their minds and spirits. Just as your body responds when a doctor thumps your knee to check your reflexes, or just as when you laugh when you're being tickled,

children's bodies respond to both non-sexual and sexual touch. Children who experienced emotionally manipulative sexual abuse may feel like their bodies betrayed them by responding in this way—they may hate their bodies for this betrayal. Victims of more physically violent abuse may hate their bodies for giving them unbearable pain. Either of these situations can result in lifelong internal wars between the victims and their bodies.

Many abuse victims cope with abuse by dissociating, "spacing out" or completely disconnecting from their bodies to the point that their only physical sensation is numbness. They may feel as if their bodies belong to someone else, or as if they are floating somewhere above their bodies, watching rather than experiencing what is happening to them.

Later on, the pain, dissociation, and self-hatred can combine in devastating ways: some victims cut, burn, and otherwise mutilate their bodies in order to feel anything at all, or to try to let out the pain inside.

Girls may be impregnated by their fathers and other abusers, even when the girls are quite young (9 or 10). Boys or girls may get sexually transmitted diseases (STDs) from the abuser. The younger the victim is, the more likely that their STDs will go untreated, possibly leading to infertility or death.

The more alienated someone is from her or his body, the less likely s/he is to take care of it. In this way sexual abuse can become a factor in many illnesses, including cancer. On the other side, some victims live their lives as physically damaged, fragile people with obsessive worries about their health.

5. **Isolation and withdrawal from people and activities.** Feeling fear and self-hatred makes victims want to hide. They withdraw inside themselves, becoming lonely and isolated. It is common for children who were doing well in school before they were molested or abused to become depressed and dejected. They are so upset inside that they can't pay attention to schoolwork or relax in play. Their grades and other interests fall off.

As adults the distrust, anxiety, and shame may leave them without any motivation, without the self-esteem and confidence a person needs to do the work, create the art, live the lives they were meant to live. They have been robbed of the gifts they wanted to give the world.

Some adults who were abused avoid being around children or decide not to have children of their own as a way to protect themselves from feeling the pain of their childhoods, or because they are afraid they will lose control and do to others what was done to them.

6. **Powerlessness, depression, and extreme passivity**. Victims may feel that any small bit of personal power they may have is false, because it didn't protect them from sexual abuse when they were young. Many of the child victims come to think that there is nothing they can do to make things any better. They completely give up hope, lose their will, and become depressed and indifferent. They are victimized in greater and lesser ways over and over again. Many sexual abusers experience these feelings of hopelessness and indifference too, but we know that both victims and abusers can, with help, change their lives and learn to take action on their own behalf.

7. **Anger.** Being sexually abused is such a horrible experience, the victims feel enraged. But child victims rarely get help to work through their anger in a healthy way. So they may act out their anger on weaker or younger children, or become irritable and intolerant, harming their families and pushing away friends. They may develop a lifelong bitterness about not being protected from the abuse by their families or by society.

Abused children may attempt to reject feeling like victims by acting like the offender. Spewing anger may temporarily make a victim feel powerful, but in the end, chronic anger defeats the one who is angry.

8. **Obsession with sex or complete aversion to it.** Some children who are sexually abused become sexualized. That is, they learn to be sexual in ways that are not normal for their age, and as adults they feel and act sexual at the wrong times or with people who either hurt them or use them. They may feel that their only value is in being used sexually. This can lead to prostitution.

Children who are sexually molested feel deep confusion about sex when they grow up. As adults some victims may want to be sexual in healthy ways, but they are paralyzed by flashbacks of images or feelings from the abuse. They may end up alone because they cannot have a normal sexual relationship.

9. **Questioning their sexuality and gender.** Many boys wonder if being abused by other boys or older men will make them gay, or if they were selected by their abusers because the abusers saw something feminine in them.

10. **Drug and alcohol use, abuse, and addiction.** Many victims try to make their pain go away by using alcohol and other drugs when they are adults, and even as children. Unfortunately, the more drugs they use, the more problems they have trying to build a secure life.

11. **Eating disorders**. Some girls and boys who are sexually abused develop eating disorders as a way of controlling something in their lives. They become bulimic (forcing themselves to throw up the food they eat), or anorexic (starving themselves, sometimes to the point where they have to be hospitalized or even until they die). Other victims may become compulsive eaters, using food like a drug to drown out their pain; or they gain weight as "protection," thinking that if they are fat, abusers will not be interested in them sexually.

12. **Perfectionism and workaholism.** To avoid feelings of shame, some victims try to be perfect at everything they do. The need to be perfect is often accompanied by strong inner criticism. Though they excel, they never feel they have succeeded. People with this method of coping may become workaholics, filling their minds with their jobs as a way to keep their pain at bay. They may be able to relate to their work, but not to people.

13. **Mental illness and suicide.** Many of the adolescents and adults in mental hospitals and many teenagers who commit suicide were sexually abused when they were children. Suicide is one of the most common causes of death in 15- to 20-year-olds.

14. **Sexual offending.** An unknown percentage of sexual abuse victims become sexual abusers. They learned at a young age that tricking, forcing, bribing, or emotionally coercing someone younger, more naïve, or weaker to do sexual touching with them was considered "normal" or "okay" by at least one powerful adult in their lives. They may act out against other children when they are only children or teenagers themselves. If they are not caught or do not receive treatment for both their offending and victim issues, they may continue to create more victims as they become adults.

For many victims, most of these effects never go away, but simply change form as they age. Entire lives are poisoned by childhood sexual abuse. No one who has been sexually abused as a child is ever the same. You may have recognized feelings or situations in this list that apply to you. Recognizing and letting yourself feel your emotions is a major step in learning empathy and preventing yourself from creating more victims.

Being raped is like getting a life sentence for a crime you didn't commit.

Rape means being forced to have oral, anal or vaginal sex against your will. As many as one of four women reports being raped after age 18. Many young children are raped. Men are sometimes raped by other men (it is estimated that as many as 80,000 men are raped every day in American prisons). Imagine how the media would react if one out of four persons were falsely accused of a crime! Being raped is like being sentenced for a crime that you did not commit. Rape victims often feel like they've been forced to serve a life sentence of fear, depression, sexual problems and relationship distress in their own personal prisons.

Myths about rape:

1. **Myth:** Rapists are healthy, lusty young men "sowing wild oats." Rape is a crime of passion.

    Truth: Rape is *always* a sign of weakness, indicating a need to exert power and control over someone else, an unhealthy willingness to ignore another person's wishes.

    Rape is not an expression of sexual desire; it is an act of sexual violence. It's about the desire for power and domination. Rapists purposely use forced sex to humiliate and degrade victims.

    Rapists can be of any age.

2. **Myth:** Women really want to be raped. After the initial shock, they enjoy being sexual with a "powerful" man. Some women act seductive and alluring to provoke rapists.

    Truth: Being raped is universally traumatic, one of the worst events that a person can experience. Why would anyone, woman or man, want to be raped?

Anyone who thinks women want to be raped is wrong.

Rapists are usually desperate, angry, insecure men.

No woman acts like she wants to be raped. Ask men how they would react to being told that they got raped in prison because they showed their chests while changing clothes. Do you believe men who dress well really do it because they want to be mugged? While people sometimes naturally want attention and admiration, an invitation to admire is not a license to mug or rape.

Most rapists select their victims because they are available or vulnerable, not because of the way they dress.

3. **Myth:** Pornography causes rapes.

    Truth: Pornography does not cause rapes. Men choose to rape. Those who think of women as sexual objects are more likely to use pornography which keeps alive the myths about rape and fuels violent fantasies. Rapists may use pornography to help them plan their attacks or to help them get and keep an erection.

4. **Myth:** Rapists rape attractive women who are drunk in bars.

    Truth: Rapists rape anyone anywhere. Most rapes occur in the victim's home. Rape victims as young as 6 months of age and as old as 90 have been identified.

5. **Myth:** Rapes occur in the summer when people are wearing fewer clothes.

   Truth: Rapes occur every time of day and night, summer, fall, winter and spring.

6. **Myth:** Rapists are mostly accused falsely by women or girls who went along and regretted it later.

   Truth: Rapists blame the victim to avoid taking responsibility for their crimes. Some victims may comply with the rapist's demands because they are in fear for their lives. Compliance is not consent.

7. **Myth:** Rapists are just men who were being sexual with a woman, but after the woman turned him on, she wanted to stop. She deserved what she got.

   Truth: Appropriate sex stops if and when *either* partner becomes uncomfortable with what is happening. Everyone has the right to stop sex at any point. No one deserves to have his or her body violated. No one deserves to be raped.

8. **Myth:** A woman can stop a rape if she really wants to.

   Truth: Some women do stop rapes by resisting, running, using self-defense skills, or figuring out how to get help or get away. Most victims are afraid of being killed or maimed during a rape, and some women are killed resisting rapes. Rapists use weapons, violence and threats to force their victims, and are usually larger and stronger. Rapists choose situations where the victims will be vulnerable.

   Rapists are always responsible for their actions. Rape will stop when rapists stop raping; victims cannot stop rape.

9. **Myth:** You cannot rape your wife.

   Truth: Every person has a right to say no to sex and to have their statement respected without fear of harm. Marrying someone does not give you rights to her body. Having sex with someone when she does not want it is not love or lust. It is violence. No longer is a man immune from prosecution for rape in the United States just because he is married to his victim.

Common, long-term traumas from being raped:

1. **Fear:** Rape victims frequently develop fears of normal activities that never bothered them before they were raped. Driving, going out in public, or talking to strangers may become impossible. Their sleep may be tormented. For months they may be terrified that they have been infected with the deadly AIDS virus. These fears often result in victims leaving jobs, avoiding family and friends, or moving. Some of these fears continue imprisoning a victim for years after the assault.

2. **Sexual dysfunction:** Rape victims may be unable to function sexually for months or years after the assault, and sexual contact feels frightening or disgusting. Victims report that even if they do eventually function normally, their ability to enjoy sex is never the same as before the rape.

3. **Relationship damage:** Relationships are often destroyed by rape. Victims' partners, families, and friends often suspect and blame the victims, even though the rape was not their fault. The victims often feel ashamed. Fear and blame shatter intimacy. Friends who might be supportive at first later grow impatient and say things like, "It's time you got over that now." They don't understand how long the effects of rape last.

4. **Depression:** This is found in all victims. About half of rape victims are severely depressed for months or years after the assault. Many are suicidal, and some kill themselves, sometimes long after the rape and their testimony in court. Depression involves feelings of helplessness and a loss of pleasure and meaning in life. If you have lost the pleasure of living, even winning a million dollars is meaningless.

5. **Grief:** Most victims of rape feel a sense of grief similar to what they feel when a close relative or friend dies. They wish so hard that the rape didn't happen that they may convince themselves; this is called denial. Other stages of grief include anger, depression, and bargaining, in this case to make their lives safer. Eventually, they may come to acceptance that they have been raped and that their lives have been changed.

Chapter 2 Assignments

∽ **Do not write in this workbook** ∽

2.1 How did reading about the things that can happen to victims affect you?

2.2 How do you think being sexually abused affects a child's relationships with her/his friends of the same sex and of the opposite sex? Why?

2.3 How long are victims affected by being raped? Describe how you think that women or girls feel about themselves after being raped.

2.4 As a child, were you abused emotionally, physically, or sexually, or were you neglected? If you were, think back to how it felt. How much of what happened to you do you feel responsible for? How do you think the abuse has affected your thoughts, feelings, and behaviors as an adult? How was your self-confidence affected? Do you isolate yourself from other people or close relationships? Do you have an anger problem? If you weren't abused but your child was, answer about her or him.

2.5 When a woman goes to court after being raped, she often feels like she is being put on trial. She is verbally attacked and made to feel guilty. Why? How would you feel if you were the victim of rape and were treated like this?

2.6 Is there a difference between the rape of a 12-year-old girl and the rape of a 61-year-old woman? Is there a difference if both were *psychologically* forced into having sex? Is there a difference if both were *physically* forced into having sex? There must be some differences because 12- and 61-year-old females are very different. But there also must be many similarities, because being raped is always extremely traumatic. Think about this before you answer this question.

2.7 Sometimes a husband or boyfriend of a rape victim gets angry and won't speak to or listen to his partner after she has been raped. Why would a man act like this? What is the best way to help your partner if she has been raped?

2.8 Why would an intelligent woman not want to talk about being raped?

2.9 Television and movies make rape seem okay. Many times they show a man pushing a woman for sex until finally the woman gives in and then loves it. What is wrong with this scenario? How does seeing such a distorted picture affect you?

2.10 As someone who has sexually abused another person, what advice would you give a rape victim to help her or him with healing?

2.11   Imagine you were raped by several very big, very strong inmates in prison. (This is as close as you can get to feeling the fear and humiliation a woman feels when someone more powerful than she invades her body.) Now, answer the following questions:

a) How would you feel?

b) What would you do after you were raped?

c) What would you do if you knew who raped you and never saw them again?

d) would you do if the rapists were people you saw every day? How would you feel if they raped you every night for 10 years? (Many incest victims live through this.) What would it take for you to get over it?

e) Many men say they would not talk about being raped. Would you? If not, why not?

f) Many men say they "would kill the S.O.B.s." Why do you think that killing a man who raped you would help?

g) Do you think all men who have raped should also be killed? All the men in your treatment group?

h) If you have raped someone and found that your victim's angry older brother was coming to rape you in return, how would you feel?

i) What would you think is the appropriate punishment for a person who raped you?

2.12   Try to put yourself in your victims' place. Write out your answers to the following questions:

a) What did your victims feel physically just before, during, and after you sexually abused them?

b) What did they think just before, during, and after you sexually abused them?

c) What emotions did they feel just before, during, and after you sexually abused them?

d) What do they feel now?

e) How did your crimes affect their families?

f) Think about the social worker or the police officer who was involved with your case. How do you think this person feels, physically and emotionally, about your offenses? What does s/he think about the crimes? What does s/he think of you?

2.13   Write a letter from your victim's perspective telling what happened to her or him during and after your assault. Include what your victim thought, felt, and how she or he reacted to your aggression.

2.14   Write a statement of responsibility to your victim using the following sample as a guide. Read your letter aloud to your treatment group or therapist and ask for feedback. **DO NOT SEND THIS LETTER!** Sending the letter might re-victimize your victim. Anyone who thinks he should send the letter is probably thinking about himself and how he would feel better. The needs of your victim must come first!

Statement of Responsibility

Do Not Send This Letter!

Don't copy this letter; create your own letter in your own words.

"_____,"

[Apologize to your victim:]

"I want to tell you that I am sorry for what I did to you."

[Take responsibility for your behavior:]

"I am the only one to be blamed for what I did." *or* "It was my decision to do what I did, and you are not responsible in any fashion for my behavior."

[Describe your behavior without minimizing it:]

"It was my decision to force you to suck my penis, which made you gag." *or* "I raped you for a long time after threatening to slit your throat with a knife."

[Recognize the victim's right to be upset:]

"What I have done is wrong, and I imagine I have hurt you horribly." *or* "I can understand if you are angry at me. Your anger is justified."

[Let the victim know that you are not asking forgiveness:]

"I do not deserve to be forgiven for what I have done. I have to work out my problems on my own." *or* "What I did was very wrong and not a forgivable act."

[Help the victim to not blame her/himself:]

"Don't blame yourself for what I did. Nothing you did caused my actions." *or* "I made a decision to do what I did, and I cannot blame you, drugs, anything, or anybody but myself."

[Help the victim not blame others for what you have done:]

"Your family, society, the system, or others are not to blame for what I have done." *or* "I am responsible for what I have done and deserve all of the blame for my behavior. Nothing anyone else did invited or pushed me to sexually abuse you."

[Give the victim hope for the future:]

"I hope you will remain strong, be a survivor, and rise above what I have done to hurt you." *or* "I wish you the strength and courage to recover from my actions." *or* "I am getting help so that I will never do this again to anyone else."

[Close:]

"In summary, I wish the best for you in your recovery." *or* "Again, I am sorry for what I have done and take complete responsibility for my behavior."

"Sincerely,

_____ "

3.

How To Build Empathy

LEARNING THE FACTS about the impact of your crimes on your victims' lives is important. But knowing without caring is pointless. Feeling for others doesn't just happen; empathy is not something you will automatically feel after being in a group or reading this workbook. You have to work hard, make sacrifices, and practice.

If you genuinely understand and care about the effects of sexual abuse, you will not commit another crime. On the other hand, if you don't *want* to feel any emotion for what you have done, you are in a terrible place and have little hope of living a satisfying life. Gary is in exactly that place.

If you care about people's feelings, you will think twice before hurting them. When you care about someone, you feel affection, warmth, kindness and empathy; you can imagine how things feel to that person. Feeling empathy only for certain people, or only people you know or like, is just a beginning step toward becoming an empathic person.

True empathy is a feeling of concern and respect for all people, whether you know them or not. When you are truly empathic,

you do not exclude certain people because they are strangers, because they have harmed others, or even because they are your enemies. When you have developed

Gary

Gary was a rapist. He was caught, convicted, and sent to prison. To have something that would look good in his file, he reluctantly joined a sexual offender treatment group. During one meeting, the group watched and discussed a film about the victims of rape.

When the therapist asked Gary what the women in the film felt, Gary mumbled, "I don't know." The therapist pointed out that the women said they felt pain, shame, anger and humiliation. He asked Gary if he thought this was true. Gary shrugged and said, "Yeah, I suppose so." The therapist asked if Gary could describe how the women's pain felt. Gary glared at the therapist. "Look," he said, "I don't know or like the women in the movie, so I don't care what they felt!"

The therapist asked, "If you don't care how these women feel, when they're telling you out loud straight to your face, what's going to keep you from raping another woman you don't know or like, especially if you think you can get away with it without getting caught?"

Gary shrugged again and answered, "I don't know; nothing I guess! I just won't let myself get caught, and if I am, I'll get a better lawyer!" His answer made it clear to the therapist and the rest of the group that Gary had a long way to go to begin developing empathy.

empathy, you don't hate people or put them down because of their skin color, religious beliefs, age, or how much or how little money they have.

Work on empathizing with those you dislike.

If you are prejudiced, you aren't truly empathic. Prejudice means pre-judging people based on ideas you have about a group they are part of, not recognizing the reality of who the individuals are. When you are prejudiced, you put down, blame, or hate others; you wouldn't do that if you felt for them.

Consider religion. When you put down Catholics, Jews, Buddhists, or Muslims, you are showing that you are a narrow-minded person. To have empathy, you need an open mind. Being prejudiced about people who are as entitled to believe in their religion as you are in yours shows how self-centered you are, not how "wrong" others are.

One way to develop compassion is to learn what other people feel. Consider groups of people who are discriminated against: women, lesbians, and gay men; African-Americans, Asians, Latinos, and Indians; disabled people and fat people. Especially consider groups that you dislike.

Think about how you would feel if people jeered at you when you walked into a bar because of your background, color, or size. Would walking down the street be safe for you if you were a woman or a gay man? How would it feel to make less money than a co-worker doing the same job because you were a woman? What would it feel like to be unable to walk up a flight of stairs and have to hear people make cracks about it? Everyone wants to be respected and treated with dignity.

Practice good humor.

To encourage your empathy, look closely at your humor. Humor is great. People without it are often depressed or have no joy. Healthy humor looks at the contradictions in life and the ridiculousness of the human situation; it allows us to laugh at ourselves and to not be so tense about our problems.

Unfortunately, many people have learned to use a poisonous kind of humor that puts people down. When you make ethnic or sexual jokes that dehumanize others, it is usually about groups that you don't belong to, or you probably wouldn't think these jokes were funny. This kind of humor exists only where there is no empathy. Its purpose is to hurt, degrade, ridicule and/or humiliate a person or a group of people. Notice these words: *hurt, degrade, humiliate*. They should remind you of the description of rape in the last chapter. Dehumanizing humor is like verbal rape: if you were really able to put yourself in the place of the people being joked about, it would hurt and no longer be funny.

All of these things take time to become aware of and sort out for yourself.

Set aside time to be alone.

To cultivate empathy, you need to become aware of and respond to your deep sympathetic feelings. To do this you need some time alone every day. This does not mean you should become a loner or try to do it all yourself. It means that you need a half-hour to an hour of quiet time to reflect in addition to your homework time. Set aside this special time to devote to building your sense of empathy. Becoming empathic doesn't happen in 10 or 15 minutes, or even in two or three hours. It happens over time by cultivating it within you and practicing with others.

For your private time, find a quiet place where you will not be disturbed. If you are in a dorm in an institution, the best way to do this is to lie on your bunk during count or just before bed time. Don't lie in the position you sleep in, or you will tend to fall asleep. Pretend you are asleep, or tell the men around you that you are resting and to leave you alone.

During this private time, think about a particular event or situation you can use to enhance your empathy. It may be something you heard on the news (for example, an earthquake or flood). Think about the people affected by this event. Think about how you would deal with what they have to deal with, such as losing your home, or a family member drowning or being killed in the quake. The goal is to think about others, about their misfortune, and then to imagine how they might feel. Put yourself in their situation, in their shoes. Allow yourself to feel how they might feel. At the end of a half hour sit up and look around you to remember where you really are, and that you haven't been the victim of a flood or earthquake. Remember how the feelings felt.

Give yourself permission to feel your emotions.

Most men who have no empathy have cut off their own feelings of fear, shame, pain, confidence and joy. They think that expressing their feelings will only cost them pain or make them unsafe, and increase their problems. They may stuff their feelings so far inside themselves that they don't even know they are there. They have learned to hold their feelings in as a means of protecting themselves. Consider Harry (whose story you can read on the next page).

For Harry to develop empathy, he must learn to allow all of his feelings to occur and accept that they are all parts of himself. When Harry begins to accept his fear, weaknesses, vulnerabilities, and inadequacy, he can begin to accept those feelings in others too. You can only empathize with feelings you are willing to experience yourself. If you are unwilling to feel shame, you can't empathize with someone else's shame.

Empathy doesn't mean just identifying with the painful parts of yourself, it also means to be able to feel the strong, coura-

Harry

Harry was raped in the boiler room at school by a janitor when he was 12. During the rape Harry was terrified. He felt weak, powerless, and defenseless. He hated feeling out of control. He hated the rapist. He hated his parents for not noticing how bad he felt. They didn't even ask what was wrong. He hated it that they didn't do more to help. He hated the school where it happened.

Harry never wanted to feel so terrible again. He thought about his rape and decided the only one who did not feel horrible was the rapist. The rapist appeared strong, powerful, and in control. Harry began to identify with the rapist. He began to hate the weak, powerless, and vulnerable parts of himself and others.

It didn't take long for Harry to learn not to feel vulnerable. When his feelings of vulnerability died, so did his capacity for empathy. He could no longer feel anyone's pain. No one mattered to him but himself. He buried deep inside himself the part that felt small and scared. If any other kid got in his way, he would beat them up. As he grew older, he could no longer recognize other human beings as people like himself. He became someone who could rape and forget it.

geous parts of yourself in a positive, useful light.

Staying focused on yourself is the opposite of empathy.

Staying self-focused is the *opposite* of empathy in the long run. Being self-focused or self-absorbed means always thinking of yourself first, and others second or not at all. This kind of constant self-focus is called *narcissism*, and many sex abusers are narcissistic. It is the idea that you are the most important person in the universe, and other people and events are important only when they involve you or your reactions. One form of narcissism is shown if you are willing to steal, lie, or scam to get something you want, acts that are not only not empathic, but usually criminal. Narcissistic people have to work pretty hard at learning to be empathic.

There are subtler ways of being self-absorbed or narcissistic than by lying, stealing, or scamming other people. Look at how you react when others don't do what you want. Anger, violence, manipulation, and rejection mean you don't really care about people, you only care about what they can do for you.

Some abusers think they have the right to take what they want from others if they do nice things for them. Giving someone a gift or doing someone a favor does not mean that you deserve whatever you want in return. When you think giving to someone entitles you to sexually abuse that person, you are confusing caring with your desire for control and sex. Caring is not a trade. Empathizing is something you do without expecting a return—you care because you want to.

In order to develop empathy, you have to set yourself aside and put others first. Only you can make this choice for yourself. If you are bullied or shamed into doing it, it will not work—you will feel resentment and anger at being manipulated. But this change from focusing on yourself is important. In the past you have put a lot of time and energy into getting your needs met at other people's expense. To develop empathy, you must reverse this pattern and sensitize yourself to the feelings and rights of others. Eventually you will find a balance between yourself and others, but for now keep asking yourself, "How will what I am doing affect them?"

For example, if you call someone names, how will that affect the person? If you steal someone's property, how will it affect that person and others who find out about it? If you are having an affair and your wife doesn't know what you are doing, how will that affect her? (Don't deceive yourself, it will affect her tremendously.) Part of learning to be considerate of others is learning to change the way you have thought about your behavior in the past. If you're having trouble thinking of how these behaviors would affect others, try thinking about how you would feel if someone else did them to you. Then think about how other people might feel when you do these things to them.

Think before you act.

There will be times when you feel upset, discouraged, and angry, and your impulse is to act rashly or lash out at others. If you are heading in this direction, stop. Just stop. Stop everything for 60 seconds. Take a moment before you hurt someone with words or actions. Think about how the other person feels. If you were that person, how would you want to be treated?

Suppose you have a conflict with a male co-worker. Think about the situation from his perspective. He believes his feelings are justified. Imagine you completely understand and agree with his anger. How does your behavior look through his eyes? If you were your co-worker, how would you want to be talked to and dealt with?

Learning to think in this manner is one way to develop empathy, though it is really hard to do. It is easy to know what is right if you think only of yourself, but if you try to see both sides of a problem, and then solve the problem, it is much harder. It is also much more effective.

Share with others.

Human beings, like other animals who show concern, affection, and protection toward others, are fortunate to have the ability to share empathy. Share your thoughts and feelings with good people. They can be found anywhere: If you are in prison, seek out chaplains, therapists, counselors, and other prisoners working on improving themselves. If you are feeling lonely and depressed, down or frustrated, sad and discouraged, take the time to talk to them.

The more time you spend with healthy people and the more you share with them, the more you will learn from their reactions to you. If they are sympathetic to your pain and sadness, they will show you empathy in action. Observe what they do that helps you feel better. Listen closely to what they say. When you feel cared about, what is the other person saying or doing? What do they do to help you feel understood? Use this experience to help others feel cared about and understood.

Sharing leads to a sense of closeness with others. You and your new friends will begin to feel more comfortable with each other and trust will develop. It takes time, but eventually people will come to you for help. Often all they want you to do is listen while they talk. When you can really listen, you will find yourself caring for others and developing empathy. Real caring, real listening means *not* wondering in the back of your mind how you can use the information, *not* feeling like you have to fix the problem so they'll "owe" you emotionally or so they'll feel better and go away.

Practice compassion with people who are like you or who have issues or problems that won't tempt you to take advantage of them. These people may include family members, friends, co-workers, peers, and prisoners. Later you can expand the circle of people you help by working with community service organizations, for example, gathering food for a food bank. *Do not volunteer or work with groups of people who may be potential victims.* Avoid seeking out people who are vulnerable, such as children or people with severe

physical or mental health problems. While you are in treatment, review any proposed charitable activities with your therapist, group, or probation or parole officer before committing yourself to them. Find out about the people involved and the risk they and you may be in if you work with them. Share what you find out with your group leader, parole or probation officer, or therapist so you can evaluate the risk together objectively.

To develop empathy you must be involved with people. Practicing these skills and building trusting relationships will help you gain respect and feel safe. It is impossible to develop empathy when you withdraw from people or don't trust them. Living in a vacuum will leave you feeling empty, hopeless, and suspicious of people. Isolation kills empathy.

Be prepared for people to disbelieve you.

It can be tough if, as you change, no one believes you. Based on their past experience of your behavior, they have good reasons not to trust that your new way of relating to them isn't an act or another emotional scam. You may work to learn this new skill and do things differently, but no one trusts you. You may go back to your family and try to show them that you understand their points of view, and everyone just laughs at you. Or maybe you tell your parole officer (PO) that you understand that she or he has a tough job and you appreciate how she or he has worked with you. Though you are sincere, your PO thinks that you are trying to con her or him.

These are normal experiences for people who have broken the law, hurt others, violated trust, and are just beginning to control their deviancy. When these things happen, it is a good opportunity to practice empathy. Ask yourself how many times you have betrayed your parents, friends, wife, children or employer. Put yourself in their places. The belief and trust of others must be slowly reestablished with plenty of honesty and hard work on your part. It will take many honest behaviors to regain their trust. Even POs (who have seen men betray those they "love" hundreds of times) will begin to trust you after a reasonable period of good behavior and honest dealings.

Never expect anyone to have total trust in you when you have broken that trust in the past. One betrayal sets you back below where you started from. Another betrayal will show that your motivation to change was not strong enough, and that people's fears about you were correct. They will know that you do not mean what you say. You need to be strong and consistent in your efforts to change your behavior and prevent yourself from victimizing anyone else in the future.

Chapter Three Assignments

◌ **Do not write in this workbook** ◌

3.1   Remember a specific time and specific scene in the past when someone loved you. Don't think that s/he had to love you always or even most of the time. For example, your wife or ex-wife loved you when you got married. Your mother, grandmother, or aunt loved you at some time when you were a child. Remember how it felt to be loved in that scene. Allow that feeling to grow. Then imagine that you are giving the same love back to the person. Gradually, add more people to the scene and imagine giving love back to them. See how many people you can add without losing the feeling of love. Write about this experience.

3.2   Pick someone you have some small difficulty with, not an enemy, but someone it is sometimes difficult to be around. Begin thinking of this person and say to yourself, "Deep down, he (or she) is just the same as I am. She (or he) has fears, hopes, frustrations, difficulties, and pleasures. Underneath it all, our similarities are greater than our differences." Say this as you see or visualize this person during the day. Notice how your opinion of and reaction to this person change as you do this exercise. Write about your experience.

3.3   Write about one person you see who is having a hard time. Do not use a name, and do not use anyone in your group who may later hear what you have written. Think about this person and describe why you think she or he is having a hard time in life. Then imagine how this person's problem affects her or his job and family. Write about it without being critical of the person, simply observe.

3.4   Now think about your last victim. Using the instructions from exercise 3.3, write about the ways you think being sexually abused has affected her or his life.

3.5   Think about someone you know who has severe health problems. Try to imagine what it is like to be in her or his place. Without telling anyone what you are doing, try walking, sitting, or lying down in the same way that this person does. Put the same expression on your face. Can you understand how it might feel to be her or him and have those problems? Write about your experience.

3.6   Now think again about your last victim. Try to imagine what your victim might be feeling. Write down what you think your victim feels as a result of being sexually abused by you.

3.7 Find two newspaper articles that describe good things happening to a person. Describe how you think the person felt.

3.8 Write down five things that you say to yourself when you are angry at someone. They might be curses or bad names. Then picture someone in your mind and imagine her/him saying the same things to you. Write down how you feel.

3.9 Count the number of times in one day, when you are around people or watching TV, that you hear humor that puts people down or dehumanizes them. Keep track of the number of daily jokes you hear for a week. Make a little chart like the one that follows to show how many of the jokes you heard that week are based on ethnic background (such as African-American, Polish, Jewish, Hispanic, Chinese, etc.), how many are based on physical differences (such as height, weight, facial features, hair color, deformities or disabilities), how many are based on gender, and how many are based on sexual orientation. Are there other categories for trash humor?

Ethnic	Physical Differences	Gender	Sexual Orientation	Other

3.10 If possible, choose a place to put your immediate needs aside, write how you will do it, and then practice it daily. During meals and clean up are often good times to practice. Let others go first, and offer to do things for them. Remember that you are doing this to learn about empathy, not to look good or to get some reward (If you are in prison, consult with staff about doing this exercise). Write about your experiences.

3.11 Think back to one of the times you sexually abused someone. Describe how being self- centered and focusing on your own needs affected your victim.

3.12 Most of the time your mind is active. It is thinking about the past or the future, and having any real sense of deep quiet within yourself is pretty rare. When you temporarily empty your mind of your concerns, you can forget yourself and appreciate others' lives. Daily take 10 to 20 minutes of private time to relax and focus your mind. Pay full attention to your breathing and count each breath. Count from one to 10 and then start over. Write about your experiences.

3.13   What are six reasons that your wife, family, PO or friends may not think that you have changed for the better, even though you may have worked hard on changing? In your notebook, write about each of the six reasons.

3.14   Think back to a time when you were betrayed by someone you trusted: someone lied to you, or disappeared when you were counting on them, for example. What did it feel like? How would you feel and react if that person came back into your life and said s/he had changed? Would you trust that person? What would it take before you would believe that person?

4.

The Four Poisons

THERE ARE FOUR POISONS that kill empathy: urges, anger, twisted thinking, and denial. We begin to "poison" ourselves when we give in to our urges without regard for anyone's best interests. We harm ourselves and others when we do not cope with anger in an appropriate way. We fool ourselves and hurt others when we engage in untrue, destructive thinking about ourselves or others. And we fail to deal with our problems when we allow ourselves to deny that we have problems or that our behavior causes problems for others.

The first poison: urges

An urge is a powerful desire to get something you want, immediately, regardless of how or at whose expense. Urges go beyond basic wants or needs. You may experience urges for alcohol or other drugs, power, money, control or sex. When you don't cope well with your urges, you make yourself sicker.

When you experience urges you may begin to think, "I really need this; I can't get along without it. I deserve it." Your empathy evaporates. Your good sense disappears. You forget about the consequences

Figure 1: TYPES OF URGES	
BIOLOGICAL/NEEDS	POISONOUS/WANTS
Thirst	Alcohol/Drugs
Hunger	Power & Control
Evacuation(eliminate waste)	Deviant Sex (Rape/Molest)
Stretch Muscles	Hurt Others
Yawn (take in oxygen)	Take from Others
Rest/Sleep	Win at All Costs

and all you think about is how you can satisfy your urge. Some drug addicts will steal from their own families to satisfy their urge to get the drug and get high. The greater the urge, the greater the potential to poison yourself and damage others (see Figure #1).

As a sexual abuser, you cannot afford to poison yourself with urges to commit sexually abusive acts such as rape, child sexual abuse, peeping (voyeurism), or exposing yourself. When you feel this type of urge, almost unconsciously you begin to look for and manipulate potential victims. All you can think about is how to get this child or that woman or man to do what you want. Abusers abuse people to try to satisfy their urges, but it doesn't satisfy them. They are left feeling even more hollow and emotionally empty than before.

Poisonous urges start with a trigger. A trigger is any thought, feeling, place, situation, person, or thing that sets off an overwhelming feeling, in this case an urge. Often urges are triggered by seemingly unrelated events and unmet emotional needs.

If your boss gives you a hard time at work, it may trigger an urge for power. Your urge pushes you to do almost anything to feel more powerful than someone else. You want someone to know that they are powerless, just the way you felt powerless when your boss was criticizing your work. You may find yourself struggling with a desire to rape and humiliate a woman as a way of satisfying this unhealthy urge. If you get a

letter of rejection for a job you really wanted, it may trigger a need to be acknowledged. To satisfy this need, you may find yourself dealing with an urge to expose yourself. If you stew over a phone conversation with your father where he was disapproving, you might be triggered to assert your control by seducing a little boy.

If you are hungry and see a pizza, your hunger gets stronger. In the same way, if you are triggered and you see a potential victim or start acting out your abuse pattern by drinking, doing drugs, or using pornography, your urge for deviant sex might increase. *When you are triggered, you must stay away from potential victims!* Do whatever is necessary in order to prevent yourself from abusing others. For example, if driving is part of your abuse pattern, lock your keys in the car, or throw them down a storm drain. If going to a bar is part of your abuse behavior, instead go to an AA meeting or a movie (if your abusive behavior of choice is rape do not go to x-rated movies! If you molest children, do not go to g-rated movies or afternoon shows aimed at kids!). If going to a strip show feeds your urges, go to a library or a church. Seek help immediately. Call your therapist, a friend who will not excuse or help you rationalize your behavior, call your PO or another member of your treatment group. Do not underestimate the power of poisonous urges to wreck your progress and your life.

Figure #2: IDENTIFYING TRIGGERS	
WHAT I DID	HOW I FELT
went to work	feeling good about my project
argued with boss	felt pushed, not respected for my work
had dinner with family	hate it when my father puts me down
watched tv	enjoyed a funny show

When you get an urge, and *only when you are sure that you will not victimize anyone at this time*, do your best to figure out what the trigger is. Slow down your thoughts. Make a list of what happened in the 24-48 hours before you felt this urge (see the sample in Figure #2). Analyze the list, looking for thoughts, feelings and behaviors that prompted your negative reactions. The better you know your triggers, the less likely you are to be surprised by them in situations where it's harder for you to control yourself. Then try to address the triggering situation or meet the need in a way that doesn't harm yourself or someone else. If it is a problem at work, talk with someone about the situation. If it is a rejection, reach out to a friend who thinks you're fun to be with. If deep down you disapprove of yourself the way your father did in the conversation, start working on changing what you don't like.

If you are having trouble identifying and dealing with your triggers and urges, read (or re-read) and do the exercises in our workbook *Why Did I Do It Again? Breaking My Deviant Cycle.*

The second poison: anger

All of us experience anger; it is a normal and natural emotion. Anger can benefit us when it is used wisely as a motivation to correct problems. It can hurt us when it is repressed, or stuffed down inside. Or anger can hurt others when it is out of control (see Figure #3 on the next page).

When we stuff our anger and hold it in, it builds up, poisoning us with bitterness. Some people hold anger in for awhile and then explode from the pressure. Some never control their anger, letting it spew out onto others every time things don't go their way, poisoning everyone involved. Others use anger to try to coerce people into doing what they want. This leads to people resisting, resenting, or even hating them. All forms of mismanaged anger are poisonous.

There's a serious difference between dumping anger all over everyone and expressing anger appropriately. Dumping anger may help you feel better for a short time, but your anger will return because you haven't used it to change the situation that angered you in the first place.

Figure #3: STUFFED FEELINGS

Normal emotional flow is like having the oil system on your car working well: everything keeps moving through the system. When part of the system breaks down or the filter gets clogged, oil stops moving through the system, and the engine over-heats and might be damaged by the grit. Stuffed feelings are like having a broken oil pump or a clogged filter. When your feelings don't circulate, you get emotionally "over heated", and damage to yourself and to others results.

When you are being poisoned by anger, you stop looking at your own decisions and actions, and you blame others. When you can't see how you get yourself into problematic situations, you get angry at someone else for what you've done. You might say, "She caused this, if she had not _____*(fill in the blank)*_____ , then I wouldn't be angry."

Being critical is also part of the spectrum of anger. When you are critical of others you may think, "I know better than she does." "He is full of it." Like blame and mismanaged anger, being critical is a way of setting yourself apart from others, putting them down, making them wrong and you right. Being critical, blaming, and angry prevents empathy.

One of the most common things we say about anger is, "He *made* me angry." Others don't *make* us angry—we allow ourselves to become angry. Two people in the same situation will react differently, one getting angry, the other staying calm and thoughtful—it's a choice. When you think that your anger is someone else's problem to solve, it will never be solved, and you hand over control of your own emotions to the other person.

Think of a time when someone did something and you allowed yourself to become really angry. Right now close your eyes and look at the scene, experiencing the anger, letting it grow stronger until you can really feel it.

After you have done this, think about how you made your anger increase. You probably spoke in your mind, cursing the other person, going over and over how unfair what s/he did was. The more you talked to yourself about how the other person wronged you, and how stupid, mean, and insensitive that person was, the angrier you got. This is how you *feed* your anger.

ANGER ➤ VIOLENCE ➤ SUFFERING ➤ REVENGE ➤

Bring up the same scene again in your mind. This time, when thoughts come into your mind, stop them. Don't dwell on them, don't repeat them, and don't validate them. Just look at the scene with no thoughts. What is the difference?

Now bring up the feeling of anger without the picture or the thoughts. What happens?

When you don't feed anger, it dies.

As you become more aware of what gets you angry (your triggers), and as you begin noticing your anger as it's just starting, it gets easier to manage. Work at not letting your anger build up. Pay attention to your problems; work them out, and make things better.

Anger escalates, if you let it.

Most sex abusers have a pattern of anger that keeps them going in cycles, just like their sexual abuse cycle. You get hurt and resent the pain. As you let yourself smolder with resentment, you start thinking about getting even with whoever is around you. You think about how others have wronged you in the past. You repeat to yourself all the hurtful things anyone has ever said to you until, eventually, you take revenge verbally, physically, emotionally, or financially. The person you hurt doesn't like it and wants to get even with you, stealing something from you. You won't let someone treat you that way!

The longer it goes on, the deeper you sink into the anger cycle. Then you forget that the other person is human, you are full of hate, and you have no empathy.

If you are having trouble getting your anger under control, you will find help in reading (or re-reading) and doing the exercises in the book ***Men & Anger: A Guide to Understanding and Managing Your Anger.***

Break the cycle of anger with empathy.

When you use empathy, you break the cycle of anger. It's like putting brakes on a wheel that's spinning out of control. Using empathy in anger situations doesn't mean that you "give in." It means that you understand that both sides have problems they want to solve. It's tougher than just thinking of your own needs. Solutions that address both sides' needs actually work to solve the problems instead of setting off a personal war where everyone loses.

To begin, think about things from your opponent's perspective. Why did the other person do what s/he did? What role did you play in the person's behavior? What do you think the other person really wants (more than getting even)? How can you help resolve the other person's problem?

Next, even though you are angry, try to feel for the person, truly empathizing with that person's situation. It might be easier to do if you imagine that you actually *are* the other person.

Then, after thinking and feeling from the other person's perspective, consider what might resolve the issues that you each have. "Try on" the solution from your perspective and then from the other person's, that is, pretend that this solution was *it*, the one that would be put into action. How does the solution feel to you? How might it feel to the other person? Finally, take action.

This process can work in all sorts of situations. Suppose your new baby screams constantly. Day and night she cries. When you have no empathy, you get more and more angry at the child, and eventually you will do anything to stop her from crying. The angrier you get, the closer you get to physically abusing her because of your anger and frustration.

When you are able to look at her with empathy, you realize that she is in pain. Perhaps she has colic, is afraid and suffering. When you realize this, you still don't like her crying, but you react completely differently. Instead of abusing her, yelling or punishing her, which only makes things worse, you try to help her. You feel sorry for the pain she is going through, which is much greater than any irritation you might have from the noise.

When you have empathy, you take her to the doctor, take turns with your wife tending to her, hold her, keep her warm, sing softly to her, take her for rides. When you have empathy, you respond completely differently. Empathy changes how you live.

When you hold anger toward someone, it is impossible to feel empathy. When you are angry at your victim for reporting, angry at the system or your therapist, your wife or your parents, this resentment blocks your ability to feel empathy. Larry also started out letting his anger block his empathy, but eventually he changed his outlook.

Larry

Larry was in prison and attending a sex offender group. He was angry about being asked to look at his behavior and to take responsibility for the harm he had done. One morning Bruce, the therapist, told the group, "My car was broken into when I stopped for coffee on my way in this morning. What a pain! They got my briefcase, my wallet, the registration, and some papers, not to mention my lunch!" The therapist hoped that sharing his story would lead to a discussion on how crime affects its victims and would help the group members in developing empathy.

But Larry, who was already angry with Bruce, thought, "Great, I hope they stole his credit cards and maxed them out!" He hid the grin he felt forming. It was perfect, he thought. This 'citizen' finally got ripped off. To cover his feelings, Larry said, "Maybe the person who stole your wallet and registration needed the money. Besides, you probably have insurance, and they'll replace everything. What's the big deal?"

"Can anyone in the group help Larry understand what the big deal is?" asked Bruce.

Falani spoke up, "Look, man, you ever had your wallet lifted? Remember making all those phone calls to cancel stuff? Even if you never were the king of credit, you still have to pay for stopping checks, and replacing some stuff. Did you ever carry around pictures of your wife or your kids? All that stuff is gone. The money is part of it, but it's more than that—it's like your whole identity." Larry shrugged his shoulders. *He* didn't care. The more the group tried to explain and talked at him, the angrier and more stubborn Larry got, and the less open he was to having any kind of empathy with Bruce.

Finally Jorge walked over to Larry and picked up the notebook on the table in front of him. "Hey!" Larry yelped, making a grab for it. "That's mine!" "Yeah, so what. Maybe I'll just take a walk through here and rip out pages and pass them around. How would you feel about that?"

Bruce intervened. "Jorge, give him his book back." Jorge slid the notebook over the table to Larry. "Okay, you've got your book back, Larry, so now, how *would* you feel if someone invaded your life by stealing your book?"

"I'd hate it. I'd find out who did it and kill the SOB." Larry glared at Jorge.

"Okay, so you'd be angry and want revenge. Why are you angry?"

"It's my *life*, man. Nobody has the right. It's like having my private thoughts exposed. Everybody would laugh at me. They'd joke around at my expense. I'd have to fight a lot of people to get back my reputation. NOBODY gets in that close unless I say so."

"It sounds like you would be angry because you felt invaded, maybe even a little vulnerable."

"Well, yeah," Larry finally admitted.

"So guess what, Larry. That's how I feel," said Bruce.

"Oh," Larry said. "Truth?"

"Yeah," said Bruce. Falani and Jorge and the other group members nodded, seeing the light begin to dawn in Larry's face.

"Okay, okay, I get it. It's a crappy thing to have happen to you, and it pisses you off, and you feel invaded and vulnerable," Larry said, nodding. "I got it." He looked around sheepishly. "Hey, I'm sorry, man," he said to Bruce. "It's a stone drag."

As you read about Jim and George (on page 52), think about how their lives would have been different if they had empathy for each other's situation.

Neither George nor Jim could put himself in the other person's place and empathize with his friend. If each person had attempted to understand the other person's position, the anger would not have built up and the friendship would have not been destroyed.

Jim and George

Jim and George had been friends for years. They counted on each other when things weren't going so great. One morning Jim called George because his car was in the shop and asked him to pick him up after work. George agreed, but later that afternoon George's wife became sick. George was worried about his wife and completely forgot about Jim.

Jim had a bad day at work. He was mad at his boss and instead of managing his anger, he stuffed it. After work, Jim waited for over an hour for George and did not get to the shop to pick up his car. While waiting, Jim stewed over how badly people treat him and how no one really cared what happened to him. He began focusing all of his resentment about his boss and his life on George. By the time he gave up on George, he was steamed.

He called George and exploded. He yelled and swore and called George names. He was so angry at the situation with his boss and so full of imagined wrongs that he was not interested in hearing George's reasons for not picking him up. George was hurt. He thought Jim's anger was unreasonable and unfair. So he got angry back. George and Jim stopped being friends.

When you live violently, you can't practice empathy.

Many sexual abusers lead violent lives. Their sexual abuse and their other actions are vio lent. In learning to be empathic, you need to practice a non- violent lifestyle. Fights, both verbal and physical, are unacceptable. Violence generates more violence. If you have a quick temper and an anger problem, there are books that can help. If you are in a treatment program, see if your program has a workbook or course on anger management available to you.

The poet Longfellow wrote that if we could read "the secret history of our enemies, we should find in each person's life sorrow and suffering enough to disarm all hostility." It works both ways: Empathy encourages the resolution of anger, and resolving your anger encourages empathy.

The third poison: twisted thinking

Most of us experience cognitive distortions, or errors in the way we think, at one time or another. We use them to push our point of view or to defend ourselves. When cognitive distortions continue or become extreme, they poison our ability to function in a healthy manner.

Examples of twisted thinking include: "Sex can't hurt children." "When women say no, they really mean yes." "I deserve whatever I want." "Rape is just forceful sex; women like being raped." "It's not my fault that I forced her into sex."

As you will see on the next page, Howard's twisted thinking allowed him to believe that his gifts should be repaid *by a 10-year-old* with sex, that it was an even exchange. There are always consequences for behavior that is based on distorted thinking.

What you think affects the way you feel and act. And everything you do has many effects on yourself and others. Twisted thinking can give you a false sense of being different from, more important than, or

Howard

Howard was pleased when his sister Ruth asked him to baby-sit Sarah, his 10-year-old niece. He liked Sarah and often brought her gifts just for the pleasure of giving them and seeing the girl's delight. Howard thought, "Well, it's worth it, even though the electric company bill will have to wait until next month." His gifts were more than he could really afford. After a few gifts—and a few phone calls from the insurance company, the phone company and the gas company looking for payments Howard hadn't made—he felt he was going out of his way for Sarah and started wanting something in return.

At first Sarah's kisses and hugs were enough of a reward. Howard then wanted to have her sit next to him while watching TV. Then he wanted her to enjoy his back rubs. Soon Howard wanted her to sit on his lap, even though she was kind of old for that. He began touching her on her legs, then on her crotch. Finally, he invented a game so she would touch his penis. When she refused, he got angry, and began to threaten Sarah to make her touch him.

When Sarah told her parents what was going on, they reported him. Howard was put on probation for five years and had to go into treatment for being a sexual abuser. He was served with a court order preventing him from ever seeing Sarah again.

more deserving than others. It can lead to a belief that you have a right to do whatever you want. This belief is the *opposite* of empathy.

When you think, "Nobody can tell me what to do with my dog," you choose to let your dog run free, ignoring leash laws and the damage done to your neighbor's yard.

If you decide to take a day off work without the supervisor's approval, you might be thinking, "It's my right. I've earned the time off. Who cares what they think." This kind of me-first thinking does not take into consideration that without planning the time off in advance, you increase another person's workload.

Every time you choose to harm another person, you become more cold-hearted, more arrogant, and less able to consider the rights of others. You poison your ability to feel empathy.

The fourth poison: denial

When you deny that a problem exists, when you blame others for what you have done, or when you refuse to take responsibility for your behavior, you poison yourself. Denial, blame, and irresponsibility are ways of lying to yourself and to others in order to protect yourself from consequences. However, denial does not save you. This kind of dishonesty wrecks all the work you've done to teach yourself empathy, to feel your own feelings and those of the people around you.

When you deny that you have sexually abused another person, you are lying to yourself and others. You think or say, "I didn't do it," when you know you did. If you molested a child and deny it, you are telling the child—and all the people around that child—that s/he is a liar. When people believe you are innocent when you are not, the child victim gets no protection, no care, no treatment, and no empathy after being victimized. Instead, the child gets suspicion,

Rocky and Phil

"Hey, Rocky," Phil greeted his friend on their lunch break. "Man, women are something else. I went out with this woman last night, took her to dinner at a nice restaurant, then we went to a movie she picked out. After, we went to her place. She didn't want me to come in, but I showed her who was boss. I didn't let her think for a minute that saying no was going to keep me off her. I guess I showed her, all right. She owed me, man, after all that money I spent on her." He laughed a little and shook his head, looking sort of proud of himself.

In the old days, Rocky would have congratulated Phil. After all, he'd done similar things on dates. But since he'd done time for rape and got treatment, his thinking had changed. "That poor woman! She must be feeling dirty, scared, used, stupid for trusting Phil enough to go out with him. What am I going to say?" Rocky thought. "If I don't say anything, he'll think I think it was okay, or not important enough to bother with. If he was dating my sister and did that, I think I'd want to kill him."

"Hey, wait a minute," Rocky said at last. "It sounds like she really didn't want to be sexual with you right then. Think about it. How would you feel if I did that to your sister?"

"That slut wasn't anybody's sister," Phil insisted. "C'mon, Rocky, us guys have got to stick together here."

"Look, Phil, that was rape, not sex. You were getting off on forcing her, on feeling powerful. I know. I've done the same thing." Rocky was quiet a moment. He stared off into the distance. "I've done time for it, too. I've seen men raped, and they were humiliated, used, violated. Two of them committed suicide. Women feel the same things, Phil. You hate it when anyone ignores what you want—so do women. For God's sake, man, think about how she's feeling!"

accusations, and possibly punishment on top of the abuse by you.

If you raped a woman but deny it, you are calling her a liar by saying that she is falsely accusing you. It doesn't matter whether or not you say it to her face, your actions speak louder than your words, and it is clear that you have no empathy for her. Phil was on a real denial trip when he and Rocky had lunch together the other day.

Rocky had to say *something*—even if he remained silent when hearing the story, that's all it takes for bad actions and attitudes to continue. It wasn't enough for Rocky to understand how the woman would feel—he felt strongly enough that he had to take action by confronting Phil and encouraging him to at least apologize to the woman.

Many sex abusers say that they really didn't believe that they were doing anything wrong, or they say they didn't hurt the people they sexually abused. One way to test your honesty is to look at whether you told others about what you were doing. If you felt good about sexually abusing others, if you thought there was nothing wrong with what you did, you would tell others about your behavior. Even sex abusers who brag about their sexual crimes as a way to gain respect or power in a gang or group would never tell honest people or people outside the gang.

When sex abusers try to look good they say, "I didn't do anything to hide it." However, they didn't come forward to help their victims either; they pretended that nothing happened and hoped no one would catch them. Would you have sexually abused your victim if you knew the police would find out? The answer is no. You knew what you were doing was wrong. When you try to cover up your behavior, you are in denial.

Unless you take full responsibility for your sexual offense, you are in denial. Your denial may take the form of any one or several of the statements listed under Types of Denial on the page 56.

All types of denial affect your ability to be empathic. Denying the frequency or intrusiveness of your sexually abusive behavior lets you deny the harm you have brought to your victims. Minimizing your actions lets you pretend that your victims didn't suffer. Denying harm to your victims prevents you from seeing your victims as people with feelings and thoughts about what happened to them. Denying that they have feelings and thoughts lets you think of them—if you think of them at all—as things that can be used, instead of people, like you, who have feelings, who hurt when others abuse them. If you believe your victims did not suffer, you are less likely to feel anything for them and less likely to want to change.

Antidotes to the four poisons

Just as there are antidotes (substances that counteract the dangerous effects) to physi-cal poisons, there are antidotes to emotional poisons. To develop empathy, you must overcome your urges, manage your anger, interrupt your twisted thinking, and trans-form all levels of denial by taking responsi-bility for your behavior. As your denial lessens, your cognitive distortions break down, and your urges will not seem as exciting and desirable. With work, your anger will become more manageable. With these changes, your understanding of the effects of your actions will increase, and your empathy will grow.

If you have not already done so, you can begin this work by reading and doing the exercises in our other workbooks for sexual abusers:

1) *Who Am I & Why Am I in Treatment*
2) *Why Did I Do It Again? Understanding My Cycle of Problem Behaviors*
3) *How Can I Stop? Breaking My Deviant Cycle.*

A fourth helpful book is not just for sex-ual abusers, but for all men who have hurt someone or destroyed property because of their anger: *Men & Anger: A Guide to Understanding and Managing Your Anger.* All four of these books will help you build up your resistance to the four poisons by helping you find and use your own specific antidotes.

Types of Denial[1]

Complete Denial of Responsibility:

> I didn't do it.
>
> I was out of the state at the time.
>
> She's lying; she made it up.
>
> I was drunk. I must have blacked out.

Denial of Intent:

> It just happened.
>
> I didn't want it to happen, things got out of control.

Denial of Harm:

> I did it, but it didn't hurt him, certainly not as bad as they say.
>
> It didn't hurt me when I was abused.

Denial of Frequency:

> I did it, but only a few times, not the 20 times he says.

Denial of Intrusiveness:

> I only fondled her.
>
> I didn't sodomize him, no matter what he says.

Denial of Fantasy:

> I abused children, but the thought of it disgusts me.
>
> I never get turned on when I think about it.

Making Excuses:

> I was teaching him about sex.
>
> I was checking her out because she said she hurt down there.

Minimization of Behavior:

> I only touched her.
>
> It wasn't a big deal.
>
> I only put the "tip" in.

Taking Responsibility: Antidotes to Denial

Admission, Acceptance of Problem:

> I did it. It's my responsibility.
>
> I did everything s/he said I did, and there are things I did that s/he didn't mention.
>
> I'm sure I hurt him, though I don't know how badly.
>
> Even though I hurt him, sometimes I still get turned on when I think about it.

Chapter Four Assignments

⟲ Do not write in this workbook ⟳

NOTE: Some of these exercises are difficult and may require help from your therapist or counselor.

4.1 Write down examples of your poisonous urges and how these urges have hurt:
a) your victims,
b) your family and friends,
c) you.

4.2 For the next week make a list of any deviant urges you feel or experience. For each urge you list, describe:
a) how long the urge lasted,
b) what you did or could have done, to make it stronger,
c) what you did or could have done, to make it weaker.

4.3 What is something healthy and good that you could start desiring? (This could be a positive urge.)

4.4 Below anger is always fear. Write down three things that make you angry, and then think about what the underlying fears might be. Write about how fear and anger decrease the likelihood that you will feel empathy.

4.5 Describe how you have dealt with your anger in the past. What are signs that you're beginning to feel angry?

4.6 Make a plan for lessening the intensity of your anger. Try out your ideas three times this week, and write about the results.

4.7 List 10 things you have blamed others for recently. Write about what happens, what it feels like, when you try not to blame them?

4.8 List three people you have criticized recently. Then write a statement appreciating each of these people. How do you feel?

4.9 Find out what a "time out" is. Ask people who have worked on their anger, been in groups, or read about anger management. Write down the details. Why is a time out an effective way to deal with anger?

4.10 Try making friends with an enemy: Close your eyes and practice this visual imagery. Visualize your friends all around you. (Notice who comes into your mind.) Then imagine that an enemy is in front of you. Visualize all of his or her negative, angry feelings as smoke billowing around you but not choking you. Visualize sending him or her good will and kindness as glowing light. Imagine the person surrounded by beautiful light. Do this every day. Write about how you feel and describe any real-life interactions you have with this person.

The leader of Tibetan Buddhists, the Dalai Lama, practices this meditation daily. He works internationally to save his people from "my friends, the enemy," those who have taken over his country. Because of his practice, he has been able to work effectively for his country without causing more harm and violence in the world.

4.11 Think about what it's like to be a police officer, the one who arrested you. Consider all of the people they have to deal with, the criminals, the media. Think of the paperwork, the bureaucracy. Write down how you think you might act if you were an officer who had to arrest a sex offender who had harmed many women and children.

4.12 When your life is chaotic and out of control, you're more likely to have cognitive distortions. When you look back on your life, you can see where your distorted thoughts affected what you did. (The cause and effect relationship may not have been clear at the time.) Write down the twisted thinking that led to sexually abusing your victim. As you do this assignment, think about how your cognitive distortions affected:

a) Your finances.

b) Your job.

c) Your social life.

d) Your self-esteem.

e) Your drug and alcohol use.

f) Your marriage or relationship.

g) Your health.

h) Your appearance. (Did you keep yourself up? What did you look like to other people?)

i) Your emotional and mental state.

4.13 How did the cognitive distortions you listed in assignment 4.12 affect your ability to have empathy?

4.14 How did your feelings and the poisonous urges you experienced at the time of your crime get in the way of your thinking or feeling anything for the victim?

4.15   Using the newspaper, radio, tv, or other media source, find two articles or stories about crimes that have been committed. Then write what you think the offender may have been thinking and how you think the victim was affected.

4.16   Write down examples of the denial you have used with each of the following people: your parents, your spouse, your children, your friends, your victims, the authorities.

4.17   Write the opposite of each of your denial statements from 4.16. Compare how you acted differently when you were in denial with how you acted, or would act, when not in denial.

4.18   Write about a time in the past when something bad happened to you and no one would listen to or believe you. How did you feel?

5.

Compassionate Action

EMPATHY IS FEELING FOR OTHER PEOPLE. But it is possible to feel for others and then dismiss them. The step beyond empathy is compassionate action, taking action to help reduce others' suffering.

When you see a car wreck and go over to assist the victim, that's compassionate action. When you see someone stranded in a disabled car on the freeway and telephone for help, that is compassionate action. When you give up something you want in order to help another person, that is compassionate action.

Whenever there is true compassionate action, there is empathy. You help the car wreck victim because you can imagine how it feels to be in a wreck. You help someone who is sick because you know how it feels to be sick. When you see someone in pain or crying, you want to comfort her or him because you know how bad it can feel to be in a difficult or painful situation.

On the other hand, if you go to help the car wreck victim and take his wallet, that is not compassionate action. If you see a disabled car and steal the battery, that is not an act of caring. If you offer to comfort

someone in distress and then sexually abuse that person, you are acting criminally and without empathy or compassion. In these examples, you're meeting your own needs at someone else's expense.

Many sex abusers feel they are taking care of and helping the children they molest. They befriend children by giving them toys, buying them candy or food, taking them camping, to concerts, or (with older teens) lending them a car. But these opportunities and gifts are not being given out of love, empathy, or a true desire to help. They are lures, always provided with strings attached, given so the abusers can take sex. Abusers ask for trust so they can betray it, and they pretend they are making a fair deal when they are stealing a spirit. When you put yourself in the children's place, and consider the long-term effects of being sexualized and molested at a young age, it is clear that this kind of giving and sharing does not involve either empathy or compassion.

Compassionate action without empathy doesn't work. Trying to help someone without understanding his or her point of view may result in conscious or subconscious manipulation to make that person do what you want, not what s/he needs. Forcing or manipulating others is harmful, not helpful; it is not compassionate.

There is way too much pain in the world for any one person—or even 1000 people—to be able to heal it all. There is a story about a boy who saw thousands of dying starfish on the beach. He began picking them up and throwing them back into the water. A friend saw him and said, "Why are you doing that? You'll never be able to make a difference; there are too many." The boy replied, "I can make a difference to this one in my hand."

Compassionate action starts by reaching out to whoever is in need right in front of you. Is there a lonely or depressed man around? Compassionate action could be listening to him or helping him laugh. Is there someone who can't bend over? Compassionate action is picking up what she dropped. Do you have money that you think you are wasting on cigarettes? Compassionate action might be giving it to an organization that houses homeless people or works with people with lung disease or asthma.

Reassuring or comforting another, helping someone feel relief, acting tenderly toward others, being gentle with others, and being patient with others are all ways to take compassionate action.

Compassion is not a sign of weakness.

A lot of men think that if a man shows his feelings, he is soft, wimpy, a doormat. Having empathy and caring for others are not signs of weakness. Just watch men who are good fathers. They are strong and protective around children, and at the same time they are gentle and caring.

It is absolutely normal for men to have feelings, to have empathy, and to express their emotions. It is a form of twisted thinking, a cognitive distortion, to think that having or showing feelings means that you are weak. And as you learned before, twisted thinking prevents you from having empathy. TV stars like Bill Cosby and Alan Alda are known for having compassion, and they often play characters who show compassion towards others.

Compassion can take a lot of strength. Martin Luther King, Jr., Mother Teresa, and Gandhi are models of compassion, and models of strength. They knew how it felt to be put down, shunned and discarded; they dedicated their lives to making a more just world. The Reverend Jesse Jackson has spoken out strongly against discrimination, itself a compassionate act, but he started his public work in caring for, feeding, and sharing a sense of self-esteem with young African-American children.

Some firefighters, police officers, and rescue team members who help out during floods and earthquakes know about empathy in action. These women and men

Ross

Ross always remembered that it was a Wednesday, his day off, when his brother called in a mild panic. "Hey, Ross, I got a problem you can help me out with. It's school vacation, the sitter is sick and I can't take the day off work or I'll get fired. Can you babysit Mitch? Just for today?"

"Jeez, Fred, I don't know. I'd like to help out. Can't you take him over to his mother's?"

"Debra's in the hospital having her gall bladder out," Fred told him. "That's why I've got him in the first place. C'mon man, how hard could it be hanging out with your own 6-year-old nephew for one day? I thought you liked kids. I thought you especially liked Mitch. Besides, you owe me for that time I pulled your car out of the ditch, remember?"

Ross knew it was all true. He did like his nephew, and he did owe his brother a favor, and he really wanted to help, especially since Mitch might be scared with his Mom being in the hospital. But it was the ring of that phrase, "I thought you *liked* kids" that made him realize he had to get out from under the pressure. "Fred, let me call you back in 10 minutes." Ross did some fast thinking, knowing that being with his nephew all day alone was beyond his limit, dangerous for both himself and little Mitch. He called a friend whose 18-year-old daughter was always looking for odd jobs. She agreed to babysit Mitch.

"Fred, I'm sorry but I can't take care of Mitch. But, look, I found you a sitter for today. She's 18, and her name's Sharyn. Here's her number. I'm sorry I can't do it, but I just can't. I still owe you."

risk their lives for others. They are models of compassion and courage. That does not mean that they never feel afraid and weak; it means that they act out of their compassion.

It is compassionate to really know your own limits and to not go beyond them. In some cases, family members will try to please others too much. It is compassionate to sometimes say, "No, I don't want to do that," especially when you know that every one will suffer if you ignore your own warning signs and do what is being asked. Ross was only trying to help when he almost got into serious trouble.

In order to be truly compassionate, sometimes you will need to decide what qualities you want, the limits of your behavior, where you will draw the line with others.

Give to others.

To practice compassionate action, give. No matter how disadvantaged, put down, unfairly treated or discriminated-against you feel, there is always someone who has a much more difficult life than yours. Even if you are sitting in a prison, you are not in the middle of one of the many wars going on in the world; you are not one of the thousands of people dying from starvation.

When you care for others, giving without expectation of return comes naturally. Giving your time, listening, and paying attention are the most basic ways to help people feel better. These gifts help them feel that you value and care for them. But beware of giving advice—even when friends ask for it—because any advice ("If I were you I would …") can make matters worse. Supporting people in solving their own problems empowers and encourages them instead of giving them answers that may or may not be right for them. You can also assist people physically in ways that make their lives easier. You can support organizations that help others by volunteering to give money, labor, intelligence, or things.

The deepest way to help someone is to reduce their unnecessary fear. By reducing unnecessary fear you help people experience freedom of action, mind and emotion, while at the same time respecting their situation in life. Helping other abusers to reduce their unnecessary fears of success, of being courageous, of looking foolish, of being taken advantage of, of doing good, of being soft, of being attacked, and so on, could be the most compassionate actions you can take at this moment in your life. Freedom of the mind, to be creative, to grow in health and maturity are the most important freedoms. Being able to do what you want when you want it—regardless of anyone else—is not real freedom, especially when people are already trapped and caged by their urges, their anger, and their delusions about life.

Sometimes compassionate action can mean doing nothing. Suppose you are in prison, and there is a person nearby who talks to himself all the time. His talk is irritating and interferes with your sleep. Without empathy, all you would think about is shutting him up any way you could, yelling at him and punishing him. With empathy, you might realize that the guy is mentally ill. Perhaps he has a chemical imbalance in his brain and has no control over how he is acting. Maybe it is frustrating and embarrassing for him. Compassionate action could be simply understanding him and letting him be.

Compassionate action can be saying no, like Ross did. It is compassionate to not give a depressed friend your bottle of sleeping pills, and to tell a child you can't play with him or her. Being assertive in doing the right thing after you appreciate both sides is truly compassionate.

At times it is very hard to know how to be compassionate. Is it compassionate to spend your family's rent money to help a friend keep his electricity turned on? Is it compassionate to lend your car to a friend who needs it if you know she is unreliable? Should you give the alcoholic on the street money when he asks for it? Think about these questions and talk about them with your therapist, counselor, or group. Just giving something is not always the best way to help.

To figure out how to help someone, talk to the person and get enough information so that you can imagine what it would be like to be in the same situation. When you can see how things look from that person's perspective, and balance it with your situation, knowing how to help is easier.

To help the homeless alcoholic, think about what it is like living on the street. It is hard to lie down safely; you have to hustle for food; people avoid you; you can't get clean. If you don't want to give a lot of time or money, you can give food. You can offer to buy him a sandwich, or you can get one and give it to him. You have helped him with a basic need, haven't harmed him by giving him alcohol, and you haven't given more than you can spare.

Practice putting empathy into compassionate action by coming up with considered, balanced solutions to the other two examples (the friend with the threat of no electricity and the one who needs a car).

Learning to live an empathic life requires practice. If you have ever played a sport, you know how it works. When you want to learn a new move, you practice over and over, and over, and over, and over again. You practice until each action is automatic. Eventually you don't have to think about what to do, you know deep down what is needed, and you act appropriately.

Chapter Five Assignments

∞ **Do not write in this workbook** ∞

5.1   Define compassionate action.

5.2   List four things you could do to help people you contact in your daily life.

5.3   Write about five times in your life you have pretended to be compassionate, when you were really trying to get something.

5.4   The community has suffered a lot from your crime. It cost money. It created more fear. It deprived you of being able to contribute your work. Think of four things you could do to begin making restitution to the community. How can you make your community a better place to live? Your restitution should be a paying back to the community, not an individual. Do not contact your victim without court, parole/probation officer or therapist's approval!

5.5   Suppose you are in charge of making sure that a certain man, who beat up many people on the street and stole all that he could, did not harm anyone again. The man says he has changed and will never do anything wrong in the future, but you don't know this for sure. How can you treat him compassionately while protecting the community? Because you don't know the future, which side are you most willing to err on, his harming someone else, or his being able to control himself and change his behavior? Write out your answer and explain your reasons.

5.6   Watch a movie or read a book about rape or child abuse victims. Tell what you think three of the victims felt. What would be an appropriate way to handle the abusers? Try to see the situation from the abusers' and victims' sides. If you see it only from the victims' side, you may want to kill the rapists. If you see it only from the abusers' side, you may want to let them go free.

6.

Becoming a Better Person

MANY PEOPLE WHO HAVE EXPERIENCED difficult times in their lives have learned not to care about themselves. Instead they protect themselves by tuning out their feelings and other people, and avoiding their painful emotions. It is impossible to cut off your feelings and still have empathy. Without empathy for yourself, you cannot experience empathy for others, or take care of yourself well.

You need to take care of yourself in order to be able to do the hard work of becoming the person you want to be. Truly taking care of yourself is not greedy: it allows you to be an empathic, compassionate, active member of your community.

Balance.

What does keeping my life balanced mean? When you work at taking care of all aspects of yourself, you can create a balanced, stable life. That means not putting so much effort or investment into one part of your life that you ignore the other parts. One way to

keep a balanced life is to look at five areas: physical, intellectual, social, spiritual, and emotional. We use the diagram in Figure #4 (next page) to illustrate a balanced life.

When you put too much energy or emphasis into one part of your life, or ignore one or more parts, you put yourself out of balance. For example, if you put everything into your physical self (exercising, recreation, etc.) you would not have enough time to develop your intellectual self. You might not feel mentally challenged and as a result you might experience boredom. Boredom is often a part of the sexual offense cycle, leading to urges and ultimately to more victims.

We all have a need to feel mentally challenged, to be social and involve ourselves with our friends, to feel a spiritual connection to something, to engage in physical activities, and to experience our emotions. When we engage in all of these parts equally, we realize maximum health.

Figure #4: ELEMENTS OF A BALANCED LIFE

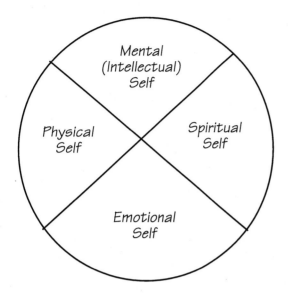

The whole is the sum of its parts.

The circle in Figure #4 represents you as a whole person. Self care involves each of these parts which makes up your entire being.

Your physical self is your body. You need to eat, drink, relax, sleep, and engage in physical activities. Your physical condition and health directly affect your intellectual self and your emotional health: How well can you think when you have a high fever? Are you happy right after falling and smashing your knee? Your physical self teaches you to care for yourself and to respect your body.

Your intellectual self needs to be active and to feel challenged. The intellect is your mind, your ability to think, learn, and use logic. Your thinking in turn affects your

feelings and behavior. Your intellectual self gives you the ability to learn about caring for others, empathy and compassion.

Your spiritual self needs you to care for and feel cared for by others, and to bond with a community. When you isolate away from others, you are faced with loneliness, and not feeling connected to the community we live in. If you don't feel part of the community it is easier to act out against its members. Your spiritual self teaches you to care for yourself and others.

Your spiritual self is your source of feeling connected. Some people are religious within a structured spiritual community—a church, synagogue, temple, mosque, or fellowship society. Others find their spirituality in nature. For some people, the spiritual self is connected to a higher power. Your spiritual self needs a sense of belonging and peace. It helps you care for yourself, others, and the larger world.

Your emotional self is your feeling self. You cannot avoid your feelings and stay in balance. We all feel a variety of emotions from pain to pleasure, anger to joy, sadness to happiness. If you close down your emotional self, you will not feel anything, including empathy. Your emotional self is directly tied to your ability to have empathy and compassion. When you stuff your feelings, you tend to experience only fear and anger, two emotions that set you onto the path toward reoffending.

Respect and trust.

You cannot care for yourself if you don't respect and value yourself. If you don't respect others, it is difficult to trust them. Without respect and trust for others, you are more likely to feel anger, suspicion, and fear than empathy.

People who don't trust others usually don't trust themselves. If you trust yourself, you do not need to worry so much about trusting others. When you learn to trust your instincts, you will often know when someone isn't trustworthy or when you need to be cautious. When you learn to trust your judgment, you choose good friends you can count on to treat you well, and you know right from wrong, as well as what is in your best interest.

Respecting others is important in developing relationships. Respect does not always mean acceptance and agreement. You can respect another person as a human being and still disagree with their ideas or beliefs.

Understand.

Understanding involves allowing yourself to be open to new ideas and new experiences. The more you understand your own feelings, thoughts, and behaviors, the more likely you are to care about them and yourself. The more you understand another person's experience, thoughts, and feelings, the better able you are to empathize with that person.

Understanding leads others to feel that you trust and respect them. Understanding helps to strengthen relationships.

Measure your progress through the four stages.

There are four stages in the development of empathy. *The first stage is becoming aware of feelings.* You recognize your feelings and allow yourself to have them when they occur. You accurately recognize other people's feelings and allow or even welcome their expression. Sexual abusers, who use people to meet their needs with no regard for others' rights or wants, often don't get to this first stage. Distorted thinking prevents them from seeing their victims as people with feelings. Lack of respect and trust prevents you from being open to feeling other people's feelings.

Once you have knowledge about feelings, you share it. If you think a friend or family member is sad, you acknowledge it by saying something like, "You look sad today," or "You've been quiet this morning. Are things okay?" If you do not practice these skills, you won't learn empathy, and you won't change. Without empathy you might be able to understand intellectually that being raped or molested can make a victim suicidal, but you won't understand on a gut level just how bad that *feels*.

The second stage in learning empathy is appreciating others' points of view. This stage includes understanding the impact of abuse on victims. You now know that sexual abuse affects victims physically, mentally, and emotionally, for the rest of their lives. Next look at the effects your sexually abusive behavior and self-centered thinking have had, and continue to have, on the lives of your victims.

Appreciating others' points of view requires that you understand their position. You make an effort or understand their needs while setting aside your needs and wants for the time being.

The third stage of empathy development is sharing others' feelings. Developing and expressing this type of emotional concern is based on understanding others. You develop the skill by putting yourself in someone else's shoes and becoming familiar with the other person's experiences. You experience the joy as well as the struggles. As you share these experiences, you begin to feel pleasure at seeing others' joy, and sorrow at seeing others' pain.

For example, you can imagine how rape affects a woman's relationship with her boyfriend, her work, and her self-esteem. You can imagine how sexual abuse affects a child's trust of adults, sexuality, and the child's sense of personal power and worth. As you imagine these situations, you feel for the person's situation beyond what you can directly see and hear.

The fourth stage is taking action on your emotional responses in ways that are beneficial to other people. Basic actions are listening and helping people, just for the sake of helping.

At this stage you can begin to make amends for all the pain you have caused. Making amends is not an excuse for contacting your victims. **Never contact your victims without permission from your therapist and your parole or probation officer AND your victim's therapist and/or a child victim's parents.** Never have contact with any of your victims unless the victim and his or her therapist have invited the contact. If you have harmed children, taking compassionate action means that you don't work with children under any circumstances. If you have raped, you do not work with women or men who fit your victim type. The best way to help people you may be tempted to take advantage of is to get away from them—fast! Instead, you help other abusers to change, or give to the community in other ways.

It's worth it.

Don't get discouraged if you have to try over and over before empathy and compassionate action feel natural to you. You have learned to do many complex things in your life, such as drive or work on your car, write or do math. You can learn to have empathy, too.

You may wonder at times if all the effort is worth it, especially when you realize how much you have hurt others. Your pain may seem unbearable, but don't give up. These uncomfortable feelings are a part of your healing process. With time you will feel better than ever. By practicing empathy every day, your life will undergo a profound change. Your life is the result of your choices and decisions. You may not have chosen to be convicted or in prison, or divorced, or on probation, but you made many decisions which made those things more possible. As you practice empathy, you can make new choices, building a new pattern for your life. A person who is warm, caring, compassionate, and strong has a very different life from a person who is lonely, self-absorbed, angry, empty, and weak. The world responds very differently to each of these people.

With effort, you will become a better person, a person who does not want to hurt others, and does not often do so. The process you go through is worth it, because you are worth it!

We wish you good luck in your treatment.

Chapter Six Assignments

∽ Do not write in this workbook ∽

6.1   People in helping professions (such as doctors, nurses, counselors, firefighters, and rescue workers) use empathy every day in their jobs (yes, some helping professionals commit sexual offenses, but they are not using empathy when they do!). Imagine being in a helping profession. Write about what it is like to be this kind of empathic professional every day. Discuss what you've written with your therapist or group.

6.2   Empathy requires understanding. Talk with someone who has problems and practice trying to understand what they are thinking, feeling and experiencing.

6.3   Empathy is an essential ingredient when teaching others or helping others to learn. Think of a skill you have (such as changing the oil in your car, writing a press release, or building a bird house) and imagine trying to teach it to your best friend. Imagine that your friend is having a hard time learning this skill. Write about how you would help your friend overcome their difficulty in learning. Discuss what you have written with your therapist or group.

6.4   One sign of empathy is your willingness to give time and attention to helping another person without expectation of gain, reward, or repayment. Practice helping someone else once a day with a task or problem. Remember to listen and not give advice. On a calendar, put a checkmark on each day that you have been able to help someone through empathy and compassionate action.

Points to remember when practicing empathy:

1.) You can't have empathy without respect, trust, and understanding.

2.) To be empathetic you must communicate empathy with others. If others don't perceive you as empathic, probably you're not.

3.) Violence and empathy are like oil and water: they don't mix.

4.) Practicing empathy will help prevent you from isolating yourself and feeling lonely, two factors that play a part in sexual offending.

5.) You cannot practice empathy while you are trying to control others and manipulate or control relationships.

6.) Empathy involves looking at a situation from someone else's perspective. If you can't put yourself in someone else's shoes and see their point of view, you can't be empathic.

7.) Giving advice is not empathy or compassion. Listening and paying attention show empathy.

8.) Trying to solve other people's problems for them is not empathy. Supporting people in finding their own solutions shows a real understanding and respect for them.

9.) It is not your job to fix everything that is wrong with the world: first, it is impossible; second, fixing problems is not empathy.

10.) Showing empathy and taking compassionate action require strength and confidence, not weakness or softness.

11.) Fear, anger, numbness, urges, and control are obstacles to empathy. Openness, communication, responsibility and accountability support empathy.

12.) Practicing empathy and compassionate action may feel artificial or phony at first—new skills often do when first used. With time and practice, being empathic, understanding and feeling how others feel, and taking compassionate action will feel more natural.